DR. CHRIS HILICKI, Ph.D.

# S.A.C.R.E.D.
# Survival

*Help • Hope*

*When Living Hurts*

Clovercroft Publishing

S. A. C. R. E. D. Survival: Help*Hope When Living Hurts

©2014 by Dr. Chris Hilicki, Ph.D.

Published by Clovercroft Publishing, Franklin, Tennessee

Published in association with Larry Carpenter of Christian Book Services, LLC
www.christianbookservices.com

Unless otherwise noted, Scripture is taken from the HOLY BIBLE, NEW INTERNATIONAL VERSION®. Copyright © 1973, 1978, 1984 Biblica. Used by permission of Zondervan. All rights reserved.

I have changed the names and identifying characteristics of individuals and places in order to maintain confidentiality and anonymity. Any similarity to actual people is coincidental. This book is not intended as a substitute for the advice of physical and mental healthcare providers and is meant to supplement, not replace, proper mental health care. The author and publisher advise readers to take full responsibility for their mental, physical, and spiritual health.

Book Cover Design by Kimberly Allen of Allen's Design Group

Cover Photograph by Emma Rice

Edited by Katina VanCronkhite

Interior Design by Suzanne Lawing

Printed in the United States of America

978-1-940262-36-9

# ABOUT THE COVER

As a child, I was always the youngest and smallest in my class. At overnight Girl Scout camp I was intimidated by the older girls' experience, imagining they had superpowers of some kind. They would good-naturedly tease the new scouts about bears in the woods and bugs in the food. I didn't know any of the camp songs, and I hadn't earned any camping badges yet. I felt alone.

One night I was particularly homesick, and my camp counselor noticed my red eyes. She said, "Come here and look at the stars with me. Do you see the Big Dipper?" I nodded yes, although I didn't. She showed me how to find it in the sky. She pointed to one small star on the edge and said, "Half of that star is mine, and I want to give you half of my half." I was amazed. I asked her why she would give me such an important star, and she explained, "I know that you are special and going to be like a big bright shiny star that brings a lot of light to people." She consoled me with compassion and gave me a special kind of attention that strengthened me to experience a better way through camp. She said, "Whenever you doubt yourself, I want you to look up and be reminded how bright you are." Like any eight-year-old, I had a million follow-up questions. I asked her what to do in the daytime when I couldn't see the stars. She laughed and said, "Well, press your fingers down over your closed eyes and tell me what happens." I told her I saw something flicker like a spark. She said, "That will do; it only takes a spark."

Sacred Survival is the spark to find your way in this world through a life that asks, "Is this all there is?" to a life that answers, "There is more." "Those who are wise will shine like the brightness of the heavens, and lead many... like the stars forever and ever" Daniel 12:3–4.

# IN PRAISE OF *SACRED SURVIVAL*

"**This is a must-read.** Chris Hilicki, writer, therapist, and healer, goes beyond writing about survival. She teaches us how to thrive, how to connect to our own innocence, a higher purpose, and how we are all sacred."

> **Tobi Fishel, Ph.D.,** *associate professor and director of psychological services at the Osher Center for Integrative Medicine at Vanderbilt University*

"Dr. Hilicki provides an **inspiring account and guide** of how to embrace, endure, and ultimately overcome the many challenges in our lives from physical to emotional. Through her professional and personal experiences she offers hope in *Sacred Survival.* A '**must-read,**' this book puts our present in plain sight, giving us a chance at healing and growth."

> **Dr. Leland Webb, M.D.,** *Major, United States Air Force*

"**A life-giving book that everyone needs to read—and a map to follow!** Whenever I go on a journey to an unknown destination, I need a guide. Not just any guide, but one who has been there, and who knows the best path. For anyone who has experienced loss, Chris Hilicki is that guide. She has not only lived it, but has the ability to take your hand with compassion, walk beside you, and lead you to hope. *S.A.C.R.E.D. Survival* is a book I will savor again and again."

> **Al Andrews,** *founder and director of Porter's Call, author, philanthropist*

"Wow. She had me at 'About the Cover.' This is a book that I look forward to **reading with a highlighter in hand.** Thank you, again. Anything that I can do to help get this book in the hands of readers would be my honor."

**G.E. (Ginny) Hamlin,** *author*

"I read lots and lots of books and carefully support only a few. I seldom presume to give a book to others unless it can truly help people heal and grow. *S.A.C.R.E.D. Survival* **made my short list of resources** to draw from and recommend before I was halfway through. No greater compliment can I offer than placing this book in the active part of my care for people."

**Stan Mitchell, Sr.** *founding pastor GracePointe Church*

"*S.A.C.R.E.D. Survival* **makes life more satisfying no matter what crisis we face.** A nationally-recognized speaker and author, Dr. Hilicki now shares her expertise and personal experience in surviving life's many challenges. Her practical and compassionate approach helps us all embrace life with intent and perspective."

**Theresa Reagan,** *cancer survivor, international cancer support advocate*

"Christians do not live in a vacuum; we face the same trials as others, yet we are called to thrive as we survive. The journey is not easy, but we are never alone. Dr. Chris Hilicki's *Sacred Survival* is **an easily read roadmap to elevate our trials from survival to Hallowed Ground.**"

**Sylvia Horne,** *cancer survivor*

"**This book is a treasure.** It's a compassionate look at the times in life that are dark and filled with despair because of chronic illness, loss or even lack of direction. It offers more than a ray of hope. Each page offers insight and inspiration to help renew, re-imagine, and restore life as a whole human being with an important and divine purpose."
> **Nancy Steingard**, *television producer and chairman, Fred Rogers Memorial Scholarship*

"Dr Hilicki gives us **six simple life-changing truths** regarding *Sacred Survival* that assist us in finding the difference between continual suffering and peace in this complex journey called life."
> **Dr. Randall Malchow, M.D.**, *medical director and associate professor of clinical anesthesiology, Vanderbilt University Medical Center*

"There are so many reasons why I respect Dr. Reverend Chris Hilicki. She hasn't just learned how to survive but how to live well. Now, in *S.A.C.R.E.D. Survival*, she is sharing and pointing us all to the tools to do this as well. To be able to live fully and wholly is within our reach if we just start to do the work. This book gives both the inspiration and proper practice to begin."
> **Melissa Greene**, *reverend, artist, American Music Award recipient*

"What **a gift of insight and knowledge.** Chris brings us such an important message. I will practice this personally and will implement the process into our home-care training curriculum so that our professional caregivers and the clients we care for feel profoundly special and loved. Isn't this what we all want? I will be giving this book as gift to many who I am in relationship with. What a support and inspiration Chris is in our survival journey."

> **Elizabeth Moss,** *president and founder of WholeCare Connections, Inc.*

"Chris Hilicki never stops amazing me. **She is the epitome of sacred survival,** of which she so insightfully writes. Now she dares to invite all to travel with her through and beyond the pain and disappointments life sometimes deals us into an unimaginable future. This book, with Chris's understanding of the power of the 'sacred practices'—particularly those of compassion and relationship—was much needed when I began an international compassion work over two decades ago. Today it's available to all of us!"

> **David VanCronkhite,** *advocate, teacher, international compassion works founder*

"In *S.A.C.R.E.D. Survival,* Chris writes passionately and compassionately. Drawing upon her clinical experience and Christian faith, she brings **a conversational tone to a daunting topic,** finding the sacred in our journey when survival means navigating painful experiences in the midst of blessing life itself."

> **Doug Herr, PsyD,** *assistant professor psychiatry, Center for Integrative Health*

# ABOUT THE AUTHOR

Dr. Chris Hilicki is a licensed professional clinical counselor, storyteller, scientist, and ordained minister living in Nashville, TN. Her mission is to explore survival in the midst of loss and uncertainty. She shares proven survival strategies for the rollercoaster journey of life, developed through personal experience, scientific research, and anecdotes. On these pages are resources to help us deal with the grief we experience when we lose the life we thought we would have (whether through death, divorce, job loss, illness, or more). Her messages, books, and lessons will help you "let go and go on" from a life that is merely bearable to one that is strong and beautiful. Look closer and discover Sacred Survival practices. Whatever your loss, move beyond the disappointment, disillusion, and despair to a life of strength and joy. Chris is a survivor of cancer and trauma. She now lives happily married, enjoying teaching, travel, music, and most of all, love and friendship.

# ACKNOWLEDGMENTS

Thank you to all who give more meaning to my life.

Thank you especially to Katina VanCronkhite, who encouraged me with her godly spirit, wisdom, incredible writing skills, words of support, and chocolate. She turned a self-help book into a sacred offering. Thank you to her beautiful Atlanta family who supported her so she could support me.

Thank you to my sister Tess who sat for countless hours in the "grandma" chairs and listened to me read and try out concepts still in development. Her acceptance and compassion inspired me to make every word count in practical and compassionate ways.

Thank you to Paul Shepherd, who has backed me up, showed up, and introduced me to the team that could turn this research and experience into a handbook and ministry.

Thank you to my best friend Theresa who is a constant presence in my heart and soul and who helped me survive the worst into the best of times.

Thank you to my friends especially connected to this topic, especially Cathy, Jill, Linda, Lisa, Judy, Nancy, Sarah, and Tobi, who shared their beliefs and expertise in survival.

Thank you to Stan Mitchell and everyone at GracePointe Church who helped me become the reverend and therapist I am today. His vision and experience have helped my survival deconstruct, reconstruct, and believe the best is yet to come.

Thank you to my big loving family across the country who supports me (and gives me lots to write about).

Thank you to my husband, who waits while I sit at my computer or in editing meetings for weeks (years) without end in sight, supporting my passions and need to serve. He keeps the window open so I can fly.

# CONTENTS

**PART I SURVIVAL PRINCIPLES**

1. The Survivor in Us All . . . . . . . . . . . . . . . . . . . . . . . . 21
   - *Our instinct for life over death*
   - *Accidental versus intentional survival*
2. Sacred . . . . . . . . . . . . . . . . . . . . . . . . . . . . . . . . . . . . 35
   - *Is this all there is?*
   - *Survival or Sacred Survival?*
3. Loss . . . . . . . . . . . . . . . . . . . . . . . . . . . . . . . . . . . . . . 47
   - *Loss is more than what meets the eye*
   - *Adjusting to change and living with uncertainty*
4. It's Physical . . . . . . . . . . . . . . . . . . . . . . . . . . . . . . . 57
   - *Pain is in our minds, spirits, and bodies*
   - *What's the connection?*

## PART II SURVIVAL PRACTICES

5. Strength . . . . . . . . . . . . . . . . . . . . . . . . . . . . . . . . . . . . . . 71
- *How do we find what we already have?*
- *Developing our strength is better than improving our weaknesses*

6. Acceptance . . . . . . . . . . . . . . . . . . . . . . . . . . . . . . . . . . . 93
- *Accept what?*
- *Creating possibilities for a life of purpose*

7. Compassion. . . . . . . . . . . . . . . . . . . . . . . . . . . . . . . . . . 115
- *How does it work?*
- *The spark before the fire*

8. Relationship . . . . . . . . . . . . . . . . . . . . . . . . . . . . . . . . . 133
- *We are created for relationship*
- *Who we are with is who we become*

9. Exits . . . . . . . . . . . . . . . . . . . . . . . . . . . . . . . . . . . . . . . 153
- *Life is a natural series of letting go*
- *What is a good goodbye?*

10. Decisions . . . . . . . . . . . . . . . . . . . . . . . . . . . . . . . . . . . 173
- *Be your best, personal, whole, and true self*
- *There's no place like home—begin there*

# HOW TO USE THIS BOOK

The practices of Sacred Survival are taken like an elevator ride that goes from one story up to another, down again, and returns to the top. One day you may feel particularly in need of going to the story about acceptance, and another day you want to stay on the story of compassion. If one doesn't provide what you want and need today, it may tomorrow. Listen to what your life is telling you and go to where you will find what you need. Ideally you will discover and incorporate all six practices. They build on each other, and they need each other. But you can start anywhere and go everywhere.

When you learn about all the Sacred Survival practices, I encourage you to come back to the beginning of the book and read it again, like it was the first time.

Strength ⇔ Acceptance ⇔ Compassion ⇔ Relationship ⇔ Exits ⇔ Decisions

# PART I

## SURVIVAL PRINCIPLES

# CHAPTER ONE

# The Survivor in Us All

The world is fascinated with survival. We tune in to watch the daily, unfolding news stories of people who are surviving hunger, airplane crashes, tsunamis, kidnappings, mudslides, disease, or a night wandering lost in a national park. When we can no longer deal with all the natural disasters and traumas of the news, we switch over to more scripted tales of survival on reality TV. We can't wait to see whose marriage will last another week or who will make it to the next round of the singing, dancing, cooking, weight loss, and cross-country race competitions. For over a decade, the Emmy-winning reality series *Survivor* has had millions of viewers cheering or jeering ordinary people trying to find food and shelter amidst island chaos and impossible tortures created to turn survivors into losers and losers into survivors. Even *Gilligan's Island*, with its forever stranded, wacky cast, is still in syndication on TV Land after more than four decades! Will they every get off that island?

The plots of the most popular and gripping movies center around surviving. Our favorite seasonal classics, such as *The Wizard of Oz, The Sound of Music* and *Ben Hur,* are actually tales of survival. Oscar winners *Schindler's List, Gone With The Wind, Titanic,* and, most recently, *12 Years a Slave,* are old and new classics that teach us what it means to endure. It doesn't matter if the characters are fictitious or historical, or whether the backdrop of their struggle is war, zombies, the apocalypse, or true evil depravity. We love them all because they deliver the triumph of overcoming amid the horror of prejudice, intolerance, and disbelief. Survivor movies outsell any other genre of entertainment, as do print biographies detailing true stories of endurance. And country music, with its soulful stories of survival, has become one of the most popular music genres.

In another realm, the word *survivorship* has been coined to bring respect to the many who have braved cancer, abuse, and trauma. Thousands of survivorship conferences are now held around the world where experts, celebrities, and neighborhood heroes teach, discuss, grieve, and cheer the victories and agonies of overcoming lives. In every arena, stories of survival mesmerize, horrify, and encourage us all at the same time. They keep us on the edge of our chair and coming back for more. Why? What is the fascination?

I believe these stories deeply resonate in most of us because there is a survivor in us all. Some of us have overcome natural disasters, while others have come through a divorce or relationship split, a grim medical diagnosis, unemployment, or the death of a loved one. Some of these experiences seem to naturally find closure; others seem to have no end, good or bad. Regardless, we are guided by an innate, God-given desire to survive. It is one of the most basic physical and psychological mechanisms that we are born with, critical to set us on a course to sustain our live.

We also love survivor stories because our culture loves winners, and survival acknowledges that a battle has been won and a winner declared. We are drawn to the winners because they seem to have one of our society's greatest and most valuable commodities: control over their fate. Or at least for the time being they appear to have outwitted or outlasted their demons, adversaries, and circumstances.

I am sure that the reason I am so interested in, and in awe of survival is because I too have known survival. It is an ongoing story that continues to change me. When I was in my early thirties, I was diagnosed with cancer and, subsequently, had recurrence after recurrence. In

> We are drawn to the winners because they seem to have one of our society's greatest and most valuable commodities: control over their fate.

its wake, I was affected with a neurological condition that interrupted the typical functioning of numerous organs from bone marrow to brain chemistry. Several times doctors told family members that my life was at risk and my death was a strong possibility.

In 2012, my heart, and life, did actually cease to beat. I was again in the hospital (St. Thomas of Nashville) and was mistakenly given ten times the amount of the medicine prescribed. My heart rate plummeted from 180 beats per minute to 18 and then to zero. I had flatlined. When people say they flatlined, it's because their EKG looks like a flat line. After my heart started, it stopped again. And then my heart started to beat. Then it arrested for the third time. When I started coming to, I sensed panic and commotion all around. I saw, directly over me, my nurse sitting on top of me beginning compressions on my heart. I heard a loud, excited voice shouting, "Clear and charge to 200!" The room was full of people in various colors of scrub uniforms. My eyes were open, but I was unable to speak what I was desperately screaming in my mind: "Stop, I'm alive!"

Eventually, the room became aware that I was gaining consciousness, and the recovery process began, just like on TV. Later, in the intensive care unit, the hospital pastor came to see me. She said, "Chris, when you were coming around, we asked you the standard reorientation questions. One of them was, 'Do you know where you are?' Chris—you said, 'Heaven, I'm in heaven.' "

The next day was my birthday, which also fell on Thanksgiving. Should I be thankful? I mean, my chest ached. My emotions were raw. My mind was trying to wrap itself around the event, but couldn't quite. Had I died? Was I going to live? Was I lucky? Was I blessed and healed? What should my prayers sound like now? What am I still praying for?

My heart literally stopped on that day and, for a few seconds, my spirit left my body. You may be reading this book now because you feel like your heart has also stopped. Every day you emotionally and spiritually flatline with painful experiences and memories of past traumas that have sucked the life out of you. You struggle to catch your next breath of hope. Your body numbs thinking that you have to live one more day like today with no possibility of relief. Like me, you are asking, "What now? Am I really alive or am I only going through the motions of life? What am I praying for? Do I even want to survive?"

> Every day you emotionally and spiritually flatline with painful experiences that have sucked the life out of you.

These are all honest and difficult questions with many possible answers, and none easy. My hope is that by the time you reach the end of this book, you will have new insight to find your right answers and take your life from bearable to beautiful.

## LEARNING THE ART OF SURVIVAL

Survival isn't just something we do; it is something we consciously or unconsciously study because we are all doing it on some level every moment. At some point it seems to transcend our entire being. I recall particulars of my own survival journey with the detail of colors, faces, and places. There are clear moments that I recall in my mind. And there are those moments that are layered in my physical body, where muscles twitch, and my skin chills in response to sounds and smells that trigger my survival instinct. Some make me smile, and others perceptively draw in my shoulders as if still protecting myself from any pain.

Spans of time lived out in split seconds arise in my mind like video pop-ups pointing out the backstory of bravery and treachery. There are moments that seem simple and indisputable and others that are inexplicable. Sometimes survival is taken for granted and minimized. We breathe involuntarily. We sleep because our body demands it. When we're thirsty, we reach, without much notice, for a glass of water. At other times survival is so glamorized and exaggerated on celebrity TV that it seems we will not ever capture its essence.

Never before has there been more of an expectation and sense of entitlement to live longer, healthier, and happier with the means and probability to do so than now. If we expect better homes, greater incomes, and higher educations than our parent and grandparents, then we expect better resources all around for an easier or more comfortable life. We've gone from surviving with fishes and nets to barely being able to live a few hours without the Internet. The merging of our pop and scientific cultures has generated a new survivor culture that has rewritten all the rules and game plans. Sixty is now the new forty, and we are expected to age gracefully (with new cosmetic lines designed specifically for baby boomers) and to begin new entrepreneurial careers instead of retiring to Florida. Decide how long you want to live, and there's a strategy to

> Like me, you are asking, "What now? Am I really alive or am I only going through the motions of life?

do it. My husband Rich says he will be content to live and accomplish his goals in seventy-five years. My sister Tess will feel cheated if she doesn't begin a new career at age eighty and outlive artist Georgia O'Keefe, who died at ninety-eight. Both are making health and lifestyle choices now so that their chances of such a survival are increased. Pick your desired lifespan and game plan, and there's a strong probability that you will achieve it.

Because everyone plays in this game of survival, a growing portion of our economy is now generated by how well a "good survival" plan is marketed and embraced. Grocery chains and retailers have created their own in-house lines of organic, "healthy" products to meet enlightened customer demand. We are saturated with articles, books, and blogs of how to eat, think, and exercise for a better life. And we have to keep reading because the rules are constantly changing: one decade proclaims salt should be eliminated; the next promotes adding more salt into your diet. One medical study says don't eat eggs; the next says eggs are a great source of protein. Women are encouraged to schedule yearly mammograms, then told they can be harmful and unreliable. Sometimes the rules of survival are hard to keep up with.

## THE AMBIVALENCE OF SURVIVAL

If buying organic to stay alive was all there was to the act of survival, life would be so much easier. As much as our society is focused on ensuring a lengthy survival, the reality of our lives tells a different story. More than half of us live with a persistent and painful poor health condition. The other half takes care of someone with a health problem like chronic pain, depression, or anxiety that just doesn't go away. And life careens out of control no matter what we do. Company downsizing eliminates our job. A drunken driver veers into our lane. An inherited gene puts us at risk for a rare disease. Our spouse leaves us with no warning.

Survival is far more than staying alive or being the last man standing. It isn't always black and white, or cut-and-dry. Unlike movies or reality TV, it doesn't necessarily come with a convenient or timely close. At best, survival is an ambivalent journey. Most survival experiences are battles of triumph versus failure, exhaustion versus determination, innocence versus guilt, and shame versus pride. It is never the end of the story. Life during and after survival can be messy, painful, uncertain, and ambiguous. You survived the car wreck, but how do you deal with the incessant pain of your broken back? Your father pulled through his stroke but can no longer talk or feed himself. You received a good divorce settlement but are filled with anger and feelings of abandonment.

Survival does not promise happy endings or a painless existence. With each reason for living, there may be another doubting it. My father questions his survival every day. Now in his eighties, he longs for heaven, He wakes up each morning and sighs with both gravity and gratitude realizing that he is still here for another day in his painful earthly existence. He reminds me that with the beauty of life may come the beast of living.

There are events in my own survival journey that have urged me to believe my place remains here on earth and others that beg me to give in to whatever the opposite of surviving is: surrendering, perishing, taking that last breath on earth—to be alive again in my heaven. My area of clinical research and psychology expertise in the field of chronic, long-suffering conditions helps me unravel the tangle of distress that often follows the emotional and physical pain in survival. But, more frequently, it complicates my life because I ponder and reflect on the undertows of our integrated health and health care. With every scientific correlation between physical, emotional, and spiritual life, there is an anecdote contradicting the connections I make between pain, depression, loss, and survival.

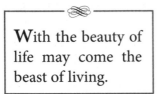

With the beauty of life may come the beast of living.

## THE SAILS OF HOPE AND PRAYER

A common response to crisis and survival in people of many religions and spiritual paths is hope and prayer. Recently, I travelled to Ephesus, Turkey and visited the home of Mary, the mother of Jesus. I passed a wall that was a city block long where people tied their prayers written on tiny scraps of paper and ragged cloth. Everywhere, I see people hope and pray. Sometimes their prayers are answered and survival goes on. Sometimes their hopes are unfulfilled, and they go on differently than they imagined.

There is a continual push and pull between hope and prayer for those seeking relief from God. Day after day, the hope to return to what life was before takes shape as a kind of prayer. When the answers and resolutions we seek don't come, hope wanes and prayers stall. It gets harder and harder to believe. The two beautiful sails of hope and prayer that once carried our dreams are now tattered and torn.

The New Testament presents us with numerous parables that contrast what was, with what could be. A particular parable, sometimes referred to as the *Parable of the Persistent Widow,* has always troubled me. It tells of a woman who persists in asking for help. Her problem wasn't going away. She went back to the one she depended on again, and again, and again. Her situation must have been lingering, enduring, and long-suffering.

Rather than a comfort, this parable has been a thorn in my side. I am that persistent woman. For more than twenty years I have returned to God through my prayers and my faith relationship while battling chronic poor health. At first glance, the parable seems to tell me to pray harder and longer, to keep keeping on until my problems go away. Yes, I believe with all my heart in the power of hope and prayer. But, after two decades, I need more than the advice to keep praying and to never give up. I'm desperate for another layer to the explanation of why sometimes the answer to my prayer is no, or silence, or that God's timing is not my timing.

What now jumps off the page when I read this parable or any of the self-help books and spiritual guides on my shelf is the absence of any promise that my prayers will be answered as I think they should be. That is why I will not attempt to explain why your prayers have or haven't been answered. And I will never tell you to pray harder and longer. I will, instead, present another possibility, one that becomes the wind to fill our sails of hope and prayer and transcend the daily emotional roller coasters, disappointments, ambiguity, and negative spirals that the mere act of surviving creates. I call this path Sacred Survival.

## FIRST THE SACRED, THEN THE SURVIVAL

The Bible is filled with many stories of people trying to survive—to find purpose, meaning, and answers to life, often in the midst of some traumatizing and horrific events. To start our journey into Sacred Survival, we must first go back to the beginning, before the survival stories, and remember the sacred story. God's first recorded acts in Genesis are acts of creation, which He blesses and declares holy. But He does not conclude His creation with man until He has first brought order out of chaos, light out of darkness, and provided everything necessary for an abundant life. In so doing, God declares both life and survival sacred. Man's life after creation is just as holy and sacred as the initial act of His creation. That desire for an ordered, light-filled, and abundant life is at the core of our very existence. From taking our first breath as a newborn baby, to enduring unimaginable pain and suffering, we are innately designed to cry out like our Creator, "Let there be…!"

Survival must then be viewed as a sacred process which can move us past declaring, "I survived!" to honestly asking, "So why is life so miserable?" Sacred Survival is an intentional process that sets life on a course from being bearable to becoming beautiful. The simplest acts of survival can be attended to, practiced, improved, and appreciated so that the life-changing journeys through sacred survival can be extraordinary.

The root of the word *survival* implies this sacred origin. It originates from the Latin combination of the words super (meaning in addition) and vivere (meaning life). The root word *sur* means over and above. So as much as survive means to live, it means to live, over and above merely staying alive. It is living over and above an ordinary existence. It is far more than how it is frequently used to exaggerate circumstances with hyperbole and embellishment, as in, "I survived my mid-term exams" or "I survived the first meeting with my future in-laws." Survival is life itself, and not only life, but abundant life, as Jesus promised. So how do we make sense of life's painful contradictions and live over and above?

## PREPARE FOR THE UNEXPECTED

As you embark on this journey of Sacred Survival, you will soon learn that what comes out of the actual practice may be different from your original intent. You see, sometimes we have a purpose for our acts, but the results are not what we expected.

For example, when I began gardening, my purpose was to end up with big, red, healthy tomatoes. That's what I envisioned. Instead, year after year I harvested tiny tomatoes with black spots, or no tomatoes at all. I didn't end up with what I started out hoping for. I did, however, end up with a wonderful experience. I made relationships with people, with the farmer's market, and even the earth. We go IN with a set purpose. We come OUT with something else—an experience.

What I am speaking to you about is this: We are called to a deeper form of survival—a Sacred Survival—where we choose not only life, but abundant life, in the midst of pain and suffering. This instinct is firmly rooted in our biological, emotional, and spiritual identity to such an extent that we will build or break our relationships with God, each other, and ourselves depending on how we pursue survival.

Everyone has either suffered in their life, is suffering, will suffer, or knows someone who is suffering and in pain. That's a lot of suffering. It was the subject of my doctoral research, and to relieve another's pain is the passion of my heart. I want to share what persistent survival looks like for me, and how it has made my long-suffering not just a little more tolerable, but sacred. As you continue to read, I am asking you to broaden your definition and practice of survival. I am asking you to consider that there is a sacred dimension to every survival experience that can free you to live on a level you never thought possible.

## THOUGHTS TO CONTEMPLATE ABOUT YOUR SURVIVAL

1. Describe your survival instinct and where you feel it kicking in.

2. What do you believe about your survival to date? Discuss when it is accidental versus intentional.

3. What are some stories of survival that give you hope? Why?

NOTES:

# CHAPTER TWO

# Sacred

## TAKING SURVIVAL FROM ORDINARY TO EXTRAORDINARY

When our survival becomes sacred, everything changes. But what is sacred and what does it mean in this context? Sacred is a word that's hard for most of us to define and often evokes visions of religious locales, relics, and rituals from hundreds or thousands of years ago. I asked over 200 people what the word meant to them and received responses like godly, reverent, and holy. When I pushed for a definition of these words, I typically got "sacred" thrown back at me. Just shows how some intangible aspects of life defy definition and clarity.

A colleague was a little startled by my pairing sacred with survival. She said it sounded religiously intimidating and might put off readers. So I began looking for places and situations where the word was used apart from religion. I've heard it used as hyperbole when people talk about something that can't be touched, changed, or challenged. "Don't meddle with that. It's sacred," they protest. Numerous movies and songs depict sacred love, sacred ground, sacred time, sacred worlds, and sacred knowledge. Other common phrases include sacred honor, sacred trust, sacred duty, sacred pursuits, sacred responsibility, and sacred rights, all of which fall outside of the religious realm. Clearly, the word infers something highly valued and important that moves the ordinary into the extraordinary. It sets a person, a location, or an object apart and has significance in all dimensions: physical, emotional, spiritual, intellectual, relational, and even environmental. There is the understanding that whatever sacred is paired with is elevated to a higher calling, reverence, and worthy pursuit. So let us first begin to revise our mundane survival as a high calling, worthy of seeking and obtaining.

The word *sacred* comes from the Middle English word sacren, which means to consecrate. *Consecrate* is another word that brings to mind religious rituals and grounds it in spiritual connotations. A monk consecrates his life to divine union and service when he joins the monastery. And when we consecrate our survival, we are connecting it back to God, acknowledging that He is there, even when our circumstances seem so devoid of His presence. We bless our survival because there is no place where we are apart from Him. Even if we believe we are living in a hell on earth, God is there. Consecrating our survival declares that nothing in our experiences has the power to separate us from the life we are created to live. It means that our struggling and suffering can emerge into something beautiful and out of the ordinary. Our survival can rise from a meager, chaotic, and solitary existence into an other-worldly reality that causes the world to notice.

Sacredness exists everywhere, in spaces and places, and

even in silence. Aspects of the sacred resonate with many people. I think I know it when I feel it and am certain that it is not reserved for only the overtly spiritual parts of life, but for my entire survival of life. Recently in Hawaii, I witnessed places where the earth met the sky and man surely lived intertwined with spirit. There, I read plaques and saw statues that used the word *sacred*. A stone carving of an empty vessel was inscribed with the words: "Holding a place for sacred." I wanted to wear that plaque around my neck even though I wasn't exactly sure what it meant. I wanted to be that vessel to hold whatever is sacred. The carving was uncomplicated, open, unadorned, existing quietly, exuding peacefulness. That's what I wanted to be—a sacred place that cannot be shaken, but is always stirring.

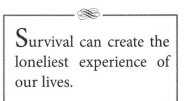

Survival can create the loneliest experience of our lives.

## HOLDING SACRED SPACE

Survival can create the loneliest experience of our lives. Sometimes it feels like no one could be going through the kind of pain that we are, and it separates us from others. The sacred shows up in the spaces of our hearts. Sacred space is that place where we come together and find ourselves in another's pain and healing or let others into our pain and healing.

I first heard the expression "holding a sacred space" when I spoke of trauma and suffering to a group of women experienced in compassion and grace. After I shared my pain, one of the women took the hand of another and said, "Let us join hands for a moment, and in silence, be united to support this woman." I held the hands of those to my left and right and waited. I waited for my experience, which I had so brave-ly shared, to be discussed, interpreted, and appreciated. In-stead, the group's leader went on to the next woman's story. I didn't understand. When would they get back to me and my story?

Before our next gathering, I asked her about it. "Chris," she said gently, "in life there are some things so horrible that words are not enough to comfort and heal. In those times what we do best is to witness and hold each other's pain so that one does not suffer alone." In love, we want to fix things gone wrong. We want to comfort the victims of hatred and terrorism. We want to console those who have lost family through illness or unexpected death. But there are times when we can do or say nothing to make it better.

These are the times when all we can do is be present for each other so no one suffers alone. When clients come to me with their horrific pain and sorrow, often from unspeak-able acts of violence, they ask, "What can you do? I'm not sure why I am even here." I respond, first, in silence, giving them all my attention. I lean into their pain as they take every breath. I offer them this: "What you have lived through and what you are reliving is too much to carry alone. Let me carry some of this pain. It's too much for one person." This is holding sacred space.

> Holding sacred space is about being present for each other when the past seems intolerable, and the future hopeless.

Sacredness can turn your survival into an extraordinary existence when you are united in the space of another's care and compassion. This isn't about a physical space, but of feel-ing and believing that you are joined to share pain and hope.

It's about being present for each other when the past seems intolerable, and the future hopeless.

## SACRED PLACE

Sacred place isn't an actual location, like a cathedral or shrine. It is a position, an arrangement, or the order of life. When you are trying to survive, life can be entirely chaotic. Sacredness exists in the calm and order of what you see, hear, and touch. Ancient civilizations believed that sacred form and design were founded in God's creation and that sacred patterns existed in the design of life found everywhere. They believed that even the human body was designed to illustrate a kind of stability that generated calm and harmony. Uniformity and symmetry in precise ratios known as Phi (1.618), or the Golden Ratio, quite literally exist from head to toe. In many parts of the human anatomy, there exists a ratio that speaks to symmetry. For example, the measurement from the top of the head to the navel, and the measurement from the navel to the floor approximate this ratio. There are numerous studies that correlate facial symmetry of people to attractiveness and greater positive reception in our society. I don't think that makes them sacred or holy, but it speaks to our instinctual universal appreciation for patterns seen in everything from human faces to plant life.

> Sacred place isn't an actual location, like a cathedral or shrine. It is the order of life when your survival is entirely chaotic.

Measurements and patterns are found all over nature, and they hold messages and knowledge for us. For example, if a flower has five petals, they produce edible fruits. If a plant has three-fold or six-fold leaves, they will most likely be toxic and require further processing in order to be used safely. These patterns have found their way into science, architecture, art, and healthcare practices. Contemporary art and sophisticated technology shows signs of patterns said to imitate God's designs of order. What does this matter? The point is that there is an appreciation for creation by a God who is holy and sacred.

Over the centuries, societies began to move away from the connection between the sacredness in creation and spirituality. The need and demand for quantifiable evidence and proof has slowly dissolved and scattered our awareness of the sacred world. Today we are more likely to be born into a culture that chooses rational explanations for life. We have grown accustomed to a defensive position where the "proof is in the pudding."

Awareness, intuition, and reverence for the sacred are gifts our generation has lost. Many exist with no real sense of place in our world, not realizing that sacredness is very much intertwined into our continual survival. God repeatedly restored order to the world, in part through the design of His creation. Recognizing this order is often an intuitive appreciation and sometimes an obsessive compulsion, but when we find a balance between order and disorder, calm and surprise, prediction and spontaneity, life will be a little more sacred.

## SACRED SILENCE

Chaos, commotion, and clamor often surround a survival experience. In a plane crash, an attack, or a fight, there can be an explosion or outburst. Even afterwards, when we are alone, our minds remain filled with the sounds of protest: "No!" "Don't!" "Help!" When we seek out the calm and stillness of a Sacred Survival, we may find our God who transforms crisis into a new way of surviving. Mother Theresa said, "Listening is the beginning of prayer." Who knew? I always thought prayer began with me talking. "Dear God, Oh God, Please, please God...." Mother Theresa also said that God speaks in the silence of the heart. She must have understood sacredness and how silence protected it.

It has taken me a long time to connect the sacred with silence. With six sisters, silence was, and continues to be, extremely rare in my family. Every moment around my kitchen table was filled with sounds of chatter, laughter, and screaming, all seemingly in the name of love. I didn't dare take a breath because someone would push their words right in between, or over my sentences. My sisters weren't responding to me, or I to them; all we wanted was to be heard.

Later, I made my living by talking. I worked on Wall Street because I could effectively spin a story that could influence the stock market. One day I was on an endless tirade to my chairman about what I can't remember. What I do remember is him gently interrupting me. He was a successful, smart, and insightful man. He said, "Be quiet for just a minute. Who beat you up in your life so that you always come out swinging the way you do with all those words?" When I closed my mouth and opened my eyes, I saw how my way of dealing with life had been shaped by unfortunate experiences with people who had a lot of influence in my life. Parents, teachers, bosses, and preachers put me in the position where I felt I had to defend myself with the only weapon I had in the world—my words. I created a habit of talking my way out of

> Sacred silence gets our attention. It is a space where possibilities live with God, unlimited by our words and noise.

and into everything, especially the physical and emotional pain I lived with.

In my earlier survival quests, I wanted answers to all my questions. I was especially demanding of God, "Why is this happening? Tell me what I should do?" In much of this relationship, God answered with silence. It was here that I learned to ask better questions and enjoy His mere presence. In silence I could hear and really feel the words, "I'm here. You are not alone." Sacred silence calms the commotion and steadies the course.

## THE DIFFICULTY OF SILENCE

In the midst of beeps, buzzes, and chirps from our iPhones, iPads, laptops, Twitter accounts, and constant alerts for voice mail, or our move with "Words with Friends," I sense a growing appreciation for silence. Perhaps it is because of the social media phenomena that there are a growing number of places for meditation and contemplation of all faiths. What am I hearing in these places? "Be still and know that I am God" (Psalm 46:10).

Being still and silent is not easy in our world. Sacred silence is more than the absence of noise. There is silence in my bed as I prepare for sleeping that is sometimes so loud I have to turn ON the TV to drown it out. At two in the morning, my mind is remembering, manipulating, and screaming at me. There is a virtual talk show going on in my mind. I am Oprah, Joel Olsten, and Whoopi Goldberg all in one. That is why a study of survival doesn't just ask about your morning. It asks, "How are you at two in the morning?"

When I force stillness on the outside, but remain busy on the inside, silence is likely to explode into annoyance and irritation. I am in pieces, left wherever I have been that day, still repeating conversations, tweaking my words, wishing I had said it differently at work, in church, to my husband, my best friend, to the driver who cut me off. I am not present here in my survival. I am still back "there" carrying on conversations.

Silence almost always comes with expectation. We are programmed to expect something for our effort, and, let's face it, silence for many is an effort. When I first started practicing silence, I had a hidden agenda. Oh, I called it purpose and intention, and even cloaked it in this new post-modern psychology strategy called mindfulness. But I was really expecting some kind of payoff: serenity, peace, wisdom, insight, unity with God, or maybe just the reassurance that I was going to survive one more day. Silence doesn't become sacred until you release it from your expectations. Until then you place a burden on it that limits its potential.

One of my clients once told me, "You are the best therapist ever!" It was a nice compliment, but what I think she was saying was, "You're the best listener ever!" My clients do the heavy lifting of therapy while I am silent. I lean into every word they say. I notice posture, eye movement, the tone of the voice, and sound of each breath. I don't speak until all their words run out. This kind of silence has timing, humility, position, and courage. It transforms from questions to acceptance, from defensiveness to receiving, and from struggle to sacred.

In the Bible, as well as other spiritual sacred texts, there is much about using our voices to make a loud noise in celebration to God. In fact, on Palm Sunday, we read that even the rocks and stones cried out "Hosanna!" In professional counseling and psychology we teach and learn the importance of finding the power of our voice. But sacred silence is celebratory and powerful, too. Silence gets our attention. It is a space where possibilities live with God, unlimited by our words and noise. It is a beautiful way to live.

## SACRED, NOT AWESOME

Words have meaning to us because of our experiences that give them context, for better or worse. I remember when the word *awesome* referred to something that was breathtaking, amazing, and astounding. When I was a young girl I heard a sermon where the minister described an awesome event. He exhaled heavily on the first syllable. It sounded like *aw-wwsome*. He went on to compare different awesome entities and events, each more inspiring than the other. Somewhere in the last decade, the word *awesome* morphed from being taken seriously to a word that is overused and means little more than something that's cool, or a little better than great. Toddlers and grandmothers alike exclaim, "That was so awesome" when describing a new flavor of ice cream. The word *awesome* has lost its significance, but the word sacred still carries, well, a sacred meaning, reserved for those people, places, and spiritual experiences that are set apart and set above. I hope we never dilute the importance of this word because it leads us to a decision to set apart our life for something amazing. Does sacredness create a better survival, or does the survival make life sacred? In that unknowing, I travel both paths simultaneously to arrive at a Sacred Survival that cannot be divided.

Survival is our most basic instinct. When we let go of the maze of thoughts that sometimes help us and other times trap us, we survive in a place ruled by our spirit. This may require a space, a place, and silence where anything is possible.

## THOUGHTS TO CONTEMPLATE ABOUT SACRED

1. Where have you seen and heard the word *sacred* used? Why do you think the word *sacred* was used there?

2. What is the connection between survival and chaos in your life?

3. Where do you go to silence the noise around you and within you? How?

4 Describe the difficulties and fears associated with silence in your life.

NOTES:

---

# CHAPTER THREE

# Loss

Survivors are usually viewed as winners and overcomers. But in real-life survival, winning often means losing. Whatever we have survived has also stolen something from us. With the obvious physical losses, such as the family home that burned in the fire or being paralyzed after a stroke, there is a cascade of ongoing emotional losses that goes along with them. One of the hardest things to do in survival is recognize and respond to what was lost.

Jacob suffers with multiple sclerosis. The doctors prepared him to expect weakness, but Jacob didn't realize how the loss of strength would impact his friendships that had been nurtured over the years in his Saturday golf games. Laura is able to control her diabetes with insulin. She was not prepared for the sadness she felt during holiday gatherings, knowing how she would miss her annual Christmas cookie exchange. If a back injury sidelines you because you can't lift that load, drive that truck, or kick that field goal, you may lose your job and, eventually, your sense of security. If you become the caretaker of a parent or spouse 24/7, you invariably lose a certain amount of personal freedom. Even the loss of your 20/20 vision or your six-pack ab muscles comes at the cost of your identity and ego.

## THE SECRET TO SURVIVING LOSS

Change is both the burden and the means of surviving loss. If you are willing to change, loss becomes the door to a new beginning instead of the ending to what was. You have to make continual adjustments in how you "do" life and how you enjoy life. Patty has arthritis. Initially, she lost some physical function in her forties. Then, in her sixties, she couldn't play on the floor with her grandchildren. In her seventies, she lost her family home because she could no longer climb the stairs. She wasn't just surviving the loss of her physical abilities; she was losing the joy and dreams of what she thought her precious golden years would be like. These losses led to her depression and anxiety. Like waves in the ocean, they kept appearing with no clear beginning but endlessly pulling her under.

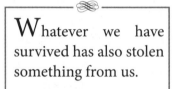

> Whatever we have survived has also stolen something from us.

Patty's physical loss was unavoidably intertwined with emotional stress. Her suffering prompted her to reassess the life she had hope for. She was able to turn her losses from a burden to a new beginning when she identified what she was really surviving and what she needed to adjust to.

Even as we make adjustments to live a good life, it still is not the life we thought we were going to live. When you have to make adjustments, it is because you had to give something up. Sometimes it is easy, and sometimes what you had to give up hurts a lot. Not everyone in your present sees what you gave up in your past. People may assume that you have a near-perfect life when they see what you look like or do. People tell me, "You look great. No one would ever know you have been sick or you're in pain." I smile, thinking, of course I look great today. You only see me when I'm feeling good because I'm in bed when I don't! I do have a good life, but there is so much more than what meets the eye with anyone suffering through chronic conditions.

What are you being forced to leave behind? Is it your job? Your marriage? Your youth? Unless you understand what you've lost, you cannot do the grief work that helps you begin again. Your survival will be superficial and you will chase yesterday. Whatever is ending remains the end instead of becoming your new beginning.

## AMBIGUOUS LOSS

Our tangible losses are fairly easy to recognize, such as the loss of physical functioning, or the loss of money, housing, or a marriage. But there are other times we incur something known as *ambiguous loss* that deals with the intangible aspects of our life like dignity, confidence, hope, and dreams. In illness or aging, ambiguous loss does not refer to death but to the diminishment of individuals' lives. A father suffering with Alzheimer's disease is still alive, but the person he has become bears little resemblance to the person he once was. The entire family now must cope with substantial physical, cognitive, or emotional loss.

Ambiguous loss can be far more devastating than the tangible losses. When your pain prevents you from playing catch with your son, you lose the pride and joy of those special father-son moments. When you lose your balance from diabetic neuropathy, you're actually losing a sense of safety.

When you lose your job, you lose your health insurance and your sense of security. These ambiguous losses fill you with an uncertainty and unpredictability that erode your identity. Yes, you are thankful to be alive, but you have been robbed of the life you had before, as well as the one you thought you would have. So we chase yesterday.

## LIVING WITH UNCERTAINTY

Problems that have no cure or resolution create an uncertainty about what can be salvaged and what will be lost. Among all the adjustments we are asked to make, the most stressful is living with uncertainty. What is most remarkable is that the deluge of uncertainty can be as debilitating as the problem itself. That's why people in remission from cancer are still anxious. They are uncertain if it will recur. The heart bypass that happened twenty years ago still haunts us because if we had a heart attack before, could we have another now? People who face the reality of their problems and accept they may be permanently part of their lives can better achieve psychological adjustment to chronic problems. They must begin to make efforts to live with an ever-changing set of circumstances imposed by their condition.

Our society values fixing things and living with certainty. Our goal is to eliminate problems. We don't do a good job dealing with the ones that won't go away. Not only do we want to fix our problems and "get over" them, we wish others would, too. We often show impatience with those who don't get better. We tire of people complaining that they miss their husband. We don't realize that yesterday's crisis lives on today, differently, but powerfully. When I was first diagnosed with cancer, I received wonderful support. I got a lot of cards and chicken casseroles from my friends. The second time I was diagnosed with cancer, people encouraged me, "Well, you beat this before, and you'll beat it again!" But no chicken casseroles. The third time I was diagnosed with cancer, some wondered what I was doing to keep getting cancer and why I wasn't fixed yet.

> Unless you understand what you've lost, you cannot do the grief work that helps you begin again.

There is such a tremendous need for spiritual guidance for those facing chronic problems. Illness, pain, aging, unemployment, and trauma have the potential to produce intense changes resulting in harmful effects on quality of life and well-being. Physical loss has psychological consequences, and psychological problems have physical consequences. The definition of chronic illness includes the words affliction, breakdown, collapse, complaint, disorder, disturbance, ache, and anguish. Emotional distress is expressed as a hurt, heartache, and pain. Long-term problems are associated with psychological and social strain that can lead to a lack of intimacy, interpersonal difficulties, depression, substance abuse, and suicide ideation.

Doctors can explain what is happening physically, financial planners can explain what's happening to the retirement plan, but more and more we are turning to spiritual and psychological leaders to guide us through the soul work of grief and loss. Physical conditions and emotional disorders are unavoidably tangled up in each other, and our heads and hearts get knotted up in depression and anxiety.

## COPING WITH LOSS

Coping strategies assist us in our survival. We may begin to cope with our stress without awareness of what we are really threatened by. If we lose our job, we may cope by networking for a new job or by protecting ourselves from financial worry by moving in with family. Either way, we are only dealing with the loss of the job, not the ambiguous losses of dignity, confidence, or ego. We do a better job surviving with coping strategies when we know and face what we have actually lost. We have to know what we lost so we can make the best choices for our survival. Our gender, culture, age, and experience with loss greatly affect how we survive. These are all elements that can help us or hurt us. One of the most important directions we have taken in finding better ways to cope with long-term problems is to go towards healthy acceptance of what we cannot control instead of relentlessly insisting on eliminating our problems.

> Ambiguous losses fill you with an uncertainty that erodes your identity. This is as difficult to live with as the loss itself.

## WHEN CHRONIC PROBLEMS LIVE OUT AS CONSTANT CRISIS

In today's world many people live with a near-constant assault of stress. A global world seduces us into thinking that a constant connection to everyone and every event, all the time, is helpful and essential. Our technological ability to communicate constantly and explicitly keeps both our joy and our tension at the front of our focus. We have diverse options to survive this onslaught of pressure. We can distract ourselves or obsess on everything. We can be sucked into a whirlpool of single-minded fixation. Some choices help us survive, but some confuse and complicate our life, and others keep us spinning and revolving, wrapped in a state of urgency without rest and clarity. Neither choice works well for long.

When we distract ourselves, we may do so thinking that

we are being brave. Distractions such as work or hobbies attempt to communicate to the world, "I can take this pain, I'm not a wimp, life goes on." Unhealthy distractions like addictions or obsessions not only reroute our attention away from the pain, they also divert the attention of those around us from talking about what makes anyone uncomfortable. When we distract ourselves from our hurts and pain, we send the mind and body a message: "This pain is going to have to really speak up for me to pay you attention and deal with you." We wait for the migraine, the heart attack, or depression to become so disabling that we have no choice but to get help. When we wait for our attention to be caught this way, we can justify the time and money to get help. Because we have created emergencies, we feel assured that others will believe how much we hurt and will rush in with help and support.

When we are sucked into the whirlpool of stress, its pull keeps us in a constant state of focus in order to keep from going under. All perspective is lost. Worse, in order to change the way we take care of ourselves or the way we are taken care of by others, the level of stress must be ratcheted up to be noticed again. Everyone has desensitized to the status quo, and we need to jolt them to regain their time and awareness. Whereas it was once startling to have couples separate, now a couple needs to file for divorce for people to pay attention. Whereas it was once on everyone's mind that you were faltering and unemployed, now they have turned their focus on the next crisis.

After I was diagnosed with cancer, I not only lost my hair, but I lost my confidence, all kinds of freedom, the certainty of what tomorrow looks like, and the dream I had envisioned of what my happily-ever-after was supposed to look like. Over time I have dreamed a new dream. I did this in the realm of building relationships with each other, myself and with God. My dreams didn't materialize because I asked God to give me new life. They didn't become a reality while I waited for that kind of prayer to be answered. Oh, that's how my survival started—but my new dreams were eventually constructed after I recognized and understood what I lost. In my crying out, I was met by God and His compassion. In this relationship my actual losses were not repaired, but my energy was restored as God carried my heartache. I could carry new dreams with the strength to execute new decisions. My longing for relief was satisfied. I stopped seeing God as not answering my prayers and holding **out** from me, to answering my prayers by holding **on** to me. That's when I began my journey into Sacred Survival.

> Go towards a healthy acceptance of what we cannot control instead of relentlessly insisting on eliminating our problems.

## THOUGHTS TO CONTEMPLATE ABOUT LOSS

1. Describe the obvious losses in your life.

2. Think about and discuss the invisible losses that you are living with.

3. How do you manage uncertainty in your life?

4. Which is harder? The change you need to make or the idea of change itself?

5. Who are your helpful and harmful role models for managing change?

NOTES:

CHAPTER FOUR

# It's Physical

## WHAT DOES LOSS DO TO US PHYSICALLY?

At our healthiest, our thoughts and feelings are woven to-gether to create happiness and harmony, or at least keep us out of a crisis mode. When our survival is threatened, they collide and may recombine into depression and anxiety. The way we process past events and anticipate future experiences might manifest as worry and despair. I believe that depression mostly lives in the past while anxiety makes its home in the future. Anxiety and depression don't only affect how we get through the day with varying degrees of energy, behavior, and mood swings; they can actually affect the brain's chemistry over time.

I think of our brain as the control tower that responds to depression and anxiety by producing more depression and anxiety, if that's what it thinks it's supposed to do or is in the habit of doing. The prevalence of anxiety and depression are so disturbing and disrupting to individuals and communities that psychologists in their offices, and parents at the dinner table discuss them, fascinated and frustrated by the mind-body-spirit connection. Obviously we study them because we seek to earnestly learn and help more, but perhaps more because they are intriguing and perplexing.

Anxiety and depression can cause physical symptoms, even when we are not aware that we are anxious or depressed. Susan came to see me for counseling because her family convinced her that she wasn't herself anymore. They noticed she was irritable, crying more, sleeping less, and losing weight without trying. Susan wasn't aware of these symptoms until she was specifically asked to recall times and frequencies of these physical symptoms. Her symptoms were actually changing the way she responded to life. She isolated herself from friends and family because she didn't want them to see her cry. This increased her feelings of loneliness, which reinforced her feelings of anxiety and depression. Yes, the relationship between the brain and our feelings is complex.

> I believe that depression mostly lives in the past while anxiety makes its home in the future.

Science confirms that depression may be triggered by either, or both, the events in your life or your biology. David had long-term stress surrounding his return from serving in Vietnam. His brain routinely coped with nightmares and reminders of his trauma. His habitual way of coping was like a big wagon wheel going round and round, deeper and deeper, until he had created a muddy rut that he was unable to steer clear from. The brain chemistry controlling his emotions was activated by his current situations. Examination of his family's history confirmed that he had neurotransmitters predisposed for developing anxiety or depression. David felt both hopeless and hopeful: hopeless because he felt his family history sentenced him to depression and anxiety that he couldn't control; hopeful knowing it wasn't his "fault" that his trauma found a home in his brain chemistry. Sacred Survival offers a rescue through the hurt to the other side of hope without the blame and guilt we often attach to depression and anxiety.

Sometimes people feel a sense of hopelessness when they learn that their anxiety and depression have a physical component. If it has an organic connection, it may create a sense that they can't control their symptoms. It may seem easier to control our situation in life than change our brain activity. However, brain chemistry can be treated, managed, and altered for a positive outcome. Neurotransmitters and hormones can be targeted for treatment with various actions from medication to behavioral practices.

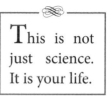

This is not just science. It is your life.

Since the 1970s, we've made progress understanding the way the brain cells talk to each other. On a typical day, our cells send trillions of messages that create excited or somber thoughts. In long-term suffering, depressive messages outpace the calming messages, and this state of imbalance is experienced as "too much to handle." This is when we begin to feel sad, terrible, hopeless, and unable to cope with life. We grasp any coping mechanism that helps us survive the constant state of fear and dread. It is normal and helpful to feel some degree of anxiety or sadness when facing a challenge and when we incur loss. It is when these feelings impair your life that you lose your Sacred Survival.

## A LITTLE BRAIN CHEMISTRY

I explained to David and Susan that their brain responds

to chemicals called neurotransmitters. I clarified that this technical word meant their moods were based on more than their will power. Neurotransmitters send messages to the body about how it should think, act, and feel. David and Susan were familiar with many of the brain's neurotransmitters because they have actually become punch lines for jokes and copy in TV scripts. They had heard the words serotonin, GABA, dopamine, and norepinephrine on commercials advertising antidepressants, and on favorite TV dramas (where there is always at least one cameo of a therapist in session with the hero or heroine.) I am amazed how these words, once strange and forbidding, are now in everyone's vocabulary and played in Scrabble. We discussed how serotonin regulates impulses, sleep, appetite, pain, aggression, mood, and even body temperature. We explored how norepinephrine affects their fight-flight response and their sleep, blood pressure, and mood. GABA helps calm their excessive excitation.

Healthy moods do not just depend on having enough of these transmitters. They also depend on a proper balance under ever-changing circumstances in our lives including age, health, and stress. There was a time when David needed more serotonin based on his high level of stress after the war. There was a time when Susan needed more dopamine as she recovered from a life-threatening car accident. As their stress levels changed, so should their neurotransmitter balances. But if their brain did not rebalance and recalculate, then they may experience anxiety or depression symptoms. More and more is being discovered about the causes and effects of neurotransmitter production and where genetics and life experience interact.

Anxiety and depressive symptoms are perpetuated by how we think. Mary was in the habit of worrying for very understandable reasons. She lived in constant fear of attack from her abusive husband. She was filled with nervous thoughts of when and where he might assault her again. Her worry created faulty reasoning. She believed she could prevent him from hurting her if she would be a better wife. She thought she might be a better wife if he would stop hurting her. This became her self-defeating and predictable circular reasoning pattern.

There is a strong physical component to our stress as well. Long-term strain correlates with racing heartbeat, shortness of breath, disturbed concentration, light-headedness, loss of appetite, sleep interruption, and more. Robin thought he might be having a heart attack when his heart raced over 150 beats per minute. He went to the emergency department three times with symptoms of shortness of breath and pain in his chest. Each time the physical exam showed no heart muscle involvement. After the third emergency exam, the doctor suggested that he consider talking to someone about possible stress in his life and a panic disorder. Robin felt embarrassed and angry, until we discussed the very real physical symptoms he was having. I told him that I believed his symptoms were real and painful. He did the right thing when he went to the emergency department in case they were signs of a heart attack. I told him that stress shows up in the body. If we ignore our stress in our mind, it will take up residence in our body. The fact that Robin was having physical symptoms didn't mean his stress was to be minimized; it actually meant that his stress was very serious and overwhelming.

Stress is complicated because most of us are not very good at connecting the dots between stress and physical symptoms. Tom worried a lot, but didn't connect the gastric reflux and stomach distress with his worry. So he didn't report his symptoms to his psychotherapist, which would have been helpful in assessing his condition. Ann reported her migraines and TMJ to her primary care physician but claimed that she wasn't worried about anything in her life. She was so used to burying her worries that they no longer showed up on her radar. If she had made the connection, her primary care doctor might have considered a different treatment plan for her care.

Our brains are beautifully complicated. The distinct ways we cope with stress show up differently in the brain. Robin's physical symptoms manifested as right-brain activity, and Mary's worrisome thoughts showed as left-brain activity. If you have anxiety, the connections between the brain's white matter and prefrontal and anterior cortex will look different compared to those who do not have anxiety. It seems that anxiety and depression do indeed activate the brain activity. Physical and emotional stress lights up our brain like no other phenomena. Brain activity matters to our survival and shouldn't be discounted. God has stored up a treasure of information in our brains that we continue to decode and reap value from, not to inflate our egos as know-it-alls, but to appreciate the power of His creation.

Ellen had sophisticated studies done to evaluate her balance of neurotransmitters. It wasn't until her treatment plan included a study of her hormones that she considered how they were affecting her anxiety and depression as well as her neurotransmitters. The two hormones include epinephrine, sometimes referred to as adrenaline, and the thyroid hormone. Epinephrine is released when our fight-or-flight system is active. With long-term strain, the ability to control the production of hormones may be damaged, leading to further impairing symptoms. The thyroid hormone appears to regulate the amount of serotonin, norepinephrine, and GABA. If problems exist with your thyroid hormones, it is possible you are more likely to develop anxiety or depressive symptoms.

If you take away anything from this chapter, it is that long-term stress associated with anxiety and depression may change the brain in ways that can cause more symptoms. It hardly seems fair that while we are already under stress from the strain of survival that we can be set back by the body designed to help us. Your survival depends on treating your depression and anxiety. If left untreated, it will affect the parts of the brain system that you desperately need for your Sacred Survival. It will affect your amygdala, which coordinates your physical fear response. It will upset your prefrontal cortex, which evaluates information and forms judgments. It will affect your locus of ceruleus, which helps determine which brain stimuli need attention. And it will disturb your hippocampus, which processes emotions and long-term memories. These are just some of the structures affected by long-term stress and loss. The longer the stress and correlated disorders go untreated, the weaker these structures appear to be. If these brain structures become damaged, they can trigger additional depression and anxiety. This is not just science. It is your life.

## THE IMPORTANCE OF PAIN

When we experience depression and anxiety, our emotional and physical pain are exacerbated. Likewise, pain can make our symptoms of depression and anxiety worse. The solution is not to numb the pain but to discover a different relationship with it that can lead to a healthier adjustment to loss. Pain, unfortunately, is demonized as an enemy to fight and eliminate, when in fact it is an unusual form of protection from God. Without pain, we have no warning that something is wrong. Without the sensation of physical or emotional pain, we wouldn't seek the improvement and correction. We might continue down a dangerous path if pain did not alert us to the fact that something or someone was endangering our life.

Pain specialist and board certified anesthesiologist, Dr. Randall Malchow, told me that Americans, like no other population, seek to numb themselves from pain. America has a unique addiction to pain "killers." We believe that science gives us the right to eliminate all the pain resulting from emotional or physical injury, surgery, or illness. Anesthetizing ourselves to our pain could create side effects that would be more harmful than the pain itself. We wouldn't have the necessary feedback to assess which treatment is helping to restore our physical and emotional balance. We wouldn't have the awareness necessary to make proper decisions for growing stronger physically and emotionally. We would actually distract ourselves from healing and prolong a state of weakness. Sadly, the journey through pain is so difficult that many go around it or away from it toward a life that is numb and settles for less.

> Sacred survival changes how we live by taking the crisis out of our chronic hurts and stress.

The patients I saw suffering from pain had one thing in common: they were at war with their hurting. Their war took the shape of anger, guilt, shame, and fear. On one particular day every single patient I saw began their doctor consultation with an apology for being in pain and for complaining of pain. They each had a version of saying, "I'm sorry for not being able to handle this pain." I was overwhelmed with sadness that we don't know how to live and cope with physical and emotional pain. We go to war with our bodies and souls, angry that they have forsaken us, or guilty that we could have done something differently. What our bodies and souls need the most is our kindness and reassurance that we are not going to abandon them but lovingly care for them and not give up on them.

Emotional and physical pains create ingrained pathways of thinking, behavior, and feeling. They work independently, but when present together, they can have exponential effect on the firing of our neurons affecting our state of anxiety and depression. In the long-term they can create a feedback loop where one reinforces the other. It may feel like a hopeless cycle of physical pain and emotional pain with no clear beginning, end, or differentiation. Narcotics, sleep, or the distraction of TV and shopping bring us temporary relief. But the side effects of such numbing agents cover up the clues intended to lead us to the corrections and adjustments to our pain and suffering. If we turn off the orange low-oil light in our car, we put off changing the oil until the engine burns out. Our minds, bodies, and spirits have become the burned-out engine. I'm not suggesting that we live in pain, but that we stay with the pain long enough to see what it is pointing to.

Mandy used narcotic pain medication whenever she felt anxiety. The problem was she didn't know she was anxious. She thought she was treating pain because her anxiety was significant enough to create chest pain and shortness of breath. She misidentified this as pain and quickly medicated herself until the uncomfortable symptoms were covered up. This is a very common coping mechanism. Over time, Mandy's anxiety was accompanied by depression, in part because her anxiety and medication created problems in her relationships. Numbing her anxiety complicated treating her depression, and it prevented her from investigating what was causing her anxiety. Without that exploration, her negative thinking, feelings, and behavior became ingrained and changed her brain chemistry. This perpetuated ongoing damaging thinking, feeling, and behavior. This cycle jams the gears in our brain until we pay attention to the pain and look at what it is pointing to. It often takes a spiritual, biological, or psychological intervention of some kind to help us pay attention and get unstuck.

## LETTING GO AND GOING ON

All of the science and explanations above don't mean anything at two in the morning when life seems barely bearable, certainly not beautiful. Letting go and going on has to start somewhere. Sacred survival changes how we live by taking the crisis out of chronic stress.

The next six chapters will open up ideas about living in the present state of suffering, without chasing yesterday or waiting for tomorrow's miracle. The past doesn't have to dictate our future. We can rewrite not just how we have interpreted it, but how it ends up—not the far-away ending, but the way it unfolds tomorrow. We don't have to throw out our memories, especially the good ones, but we can do something different with them. We can imagine a new life. Our imagination is sacred because it gives us hope. Not the kind of hope that hopes for a life the way we expected—that kind of hope can drive a man crazy. This is about living in the present while dreaming a new dream for the future.

## BEARABLE TO BEAUTIFUL

Are you a survivor? Some survivors are barely hanging on. Are you a cast-away without purpose or hope for improvement of some kind? Life becomes a grind of waking up and waiting out the day until sleep sooths our pain, numbs our minds, and merely extends our life for another day. People existing this way pray for death.

It's never too late to let go and go on from bearable to

beautiful. What is holding you back? Is your pain and suffering your only conduit to feeling alive? Is your identity tied to a bearable suffering existence? Do you want to live in the beautiful world, or is it too scary? Are you ready to let go and go on? Now is the time.

## THOUGHTS TO CONTEMPLATE ABOUT THE MIND-BODY-SPIRIT CONNECTION

1. What do you believe about the mind-body connection?

2. Describe how your spiritual beliefs impact the way you take care of yourself physically.

3. Who do you rely on for information and guidance regarding the body-mind-spirit connection? Make a list. How can you improve your access to qualified support in these areas?

NOTES:

# PART II

## SURVIVAL PRACTICES

# CHAPTER FIVE

# The Sacred Practice of Strength

L ife is hard. Period. Often by the time we find ourselves on that proverbial deserted island struggling to survive, we have already surmounted an exhausting storm of trouble and despair. That's why we begin our journey into Sacred Survival through the practice of Strength. This is not the "Keep your chin up and try harder" kind of strength. We're already too tired for that. This is the practice that pulls our existing practical and functional strengths for living to the forefront. These skills and natural abilities are what we have consciously or unconsciously already been using to navigate life in the good times and the hard times.

Some of the abilities we rely on have been easily learned and come naturally, like being a good communicator or being a peacemaker. Others are forced on us as requirements of a job or relationship, such as being a social networker when we're awkwardly introverted. Sometimes this reveals strengths we didn't know we had, but other times we are asked to use ill-fitted skills and do so for fear of losing our jobs, friends, and opportunities. Some relationships demand that we be competitive when we have no desire to one-up others with a better joke or boast of a higher salary or number of Twitter followers. Some natural abilities become habits and we are unaware they have become routine practices. The point is, our abilities are rarely intentionally used. A Sacred Survival taps into them with intention.

Sacred Survival invites us to discover and use the strengths that we already have and to use them differently. They rise to the top naturally if you let them. Given an access point they will emerge naturally and frequently because you do them so well and are more satisfied, productive, creative, and dynamic with them. You find ways to help yourself and others by using them, not for their own sake, but as instruments to change lives. Strengths, sometimes referred to as aptitudes or gifts, only improve when they are refined with practice and knowledge.

## STRENGTH COMES IN MANY FORMS

Why did I choose strength as the first practice? Obviously, the word begins with the letter S, which is the first letter for our acronym S.A.C.R.E.D. But I could have used other impacting words like sympathy, sincerity, silence, and simplicity. As I considered all the other practices of Sacred Survival, I saw that they all require strength. Strength comes in many forms. It takes strength to accept new ideas. We summon our strength, dig down, and activate our intentions to take our life off autopilot. We use different strengths to be who we are created to be instead of doing what has become comfortable. We tune into this internal force and guide it for goodness. We lavish compassion on ourselves and silence the critical voices through our strength, and sometimes we use our strength to shout them down.

Our past can literally weigh us down with sadness, hopelessness, and anger. The heaviest weight to lift is often the weight of our past. Our strengths allow us to exit the people and places binding us to our chronic crisis. Changing lanes in our lives takes enormous energy because we are turning the wheels into a pathway of resistance.

Sacred Survival asks us to uncover, use, and develop our inherent strengths. This doesn't contradict our dependence on God. He is in control and, ultimately, has our life in His hands. But, moment by moment, we live better when we discover and use the strength God has given us. The more we use our strength, the more we are reinforced to stay on the path of well-being.

> Sacred survival invites you to discover and use the strengths that you already have and to use them differently.

This first practice isn't the warm-fuzzy reassuring survival strategy you may be longing for. Instead, it is what you have needed to use for a long time. When you are equipped with the kind of strength this chapter presents, you will rest in the more obvious approaches to your survival such as finding acceptance, giving and receiving compassion, and being in supernatural relationships. But first, discover the strength-practice that will help you define your strength and use it in ways you never considered. When you learn about all the Sacred Survival practices I encourage you to come back to the beginning of the book and read about your strength, again, as if it was the first time.

## CHANGING THE COURSE OF YOUR SURVIVAL

Asking someone to change how they get through life is asking a lot. We grow comfortable and secure in our ways, making change hard. Imagine you're hanging from the ledge of a mountain with one weak hand. You believe this feeble hold is the only thing between you and death. The rescue team yells, "There's a ledge just two feet below you. Let go." You can't imagine letting go, even if your strength is failing. This grasp is the only thing keeping you alive. Letting go is too risky. What if the landing is painful? What if the rescue plan doesn't work? Your inner voice says, "Don't listen to them. You know best. At least you're alive!"

Why am I asking you to change survival strategies? Because you can survive better on that little ledge two feet below you than you can hanging by five cramping fingers from that larger ledge above. The legs you will land on are much stronger than your hand. Listening to the rescue team to change the course of survival takes the strength of humility. Humility is one of the hardest muscles to exercise. It's like the tricep muscle—small, but ugly if out of shape. Humility is crucial to Sacred Survival practices. Not because it is unassuming but because it assumes, "This could help and might be better."

This is the foundation of strength-based survival: what went "right" in your life. A strength strategy asserts that you will gain far more when developing your strength than you will by trying to improve your weaknesses. You gain more by investing in your strengths because it results in a bigger, stronger foundation to survive on. Look at it this way: you could try to do lots of exercises to strengthen your hand muscles for your next mountain climb. You could invest time and money with a physical trainer that specializes in building hand muscles. But, the fact is, those muscles are small, and all the money, time, and exercising can only develop them so much. Instead, you could develop your leg muscles so that the landing on that ledge would be a sure thing.

I asked a client trapped in depression to share his memories growing up on a lake where he enjoyed all kinds of water sports with his family. He talked about the exhilaration of water skiing. I asked him what the hardest part of the sport was. "Getting over the wake and out to the smooth water," he said. A skier can choose to stay in the rough water directly behind the boat where he is yanked, pulled, and exhausted, or he can summons his strength and head directly into the wake on either side, pushing across into calm, smooth waters. "Whoosh," my client said, leaning to the side of his chair as though pushing through the wake that threatened him today. "What's the whoosh?" I asked. He said he was remembering how good it feels to get out from behind rough waters. "I love that feeling of peace. I remember how hard it was to push through the white water, but as I got stronger, and I knew which muscles to use, I stopped falling down. I made it." He wanted to survive his current rough waters and move into the calm. He just needed to learn which muscles to use, which strength to draw on, "You can do this," I told him. "You're ready because your strength is already within you, waiting for you."

## LIVING THROUGH STRENGTH

The practice of living through our strength combines our instinct with our responsibility to actualize our potential. Our reasoning, behavior, and beliefs come together for the promise of a Sacred Survival. Operating from a strength perspective is central to many growth strategies in both the medical and the psychology world, from Aristotle's writings all the way to Carl Roger's client-centered psychology. Equally influential are our own theories of self-improvement that we've picked up at home, in school, and from hundreds of infomercials.

One compelling strength theory comes out of the work by educational psychologist Donald O. Clifton who studied what went "right" with people. From his interviews, there emerged a philosophy of using strengths and talents as the strategy for achievement. One strength strategy asserts that you will gain far more when developing your strengths than you will by trying to improve your weaknesses. This contradicts how many of us are taught and pushed to eradicate our weaknesses.

> The heaviest weight to lift is often the weight of our past.

When a child receives a report card from school, it's hard to not focus on the one "B" in the midst of the other five "A" marks. If only we could get rid of that spoiler B! In the workplace, we send employees to seminars to improve their weaknesses. Right-brain thinkers are sent to accounting classes, and left-brain thinkers are sent to creative writing classes. Type B personalities are encouraged to learn logic and project management. Type A personalities are encouraged to slow down and try relaxation techniques. Introverts worry they have social anxiety and force themselves to socialize. Extroverts are told not to be dramatic and dial it down. Do you recognize yourself in any of these scenarios?

Let's look at some of the more sensitive strengths. I've seen people depressed, anxious, and criticized because they are called "too slow" when the truth is, they are careful and deliberate. People are dejected and worried because they're teased for caring too much and crying too much when they are actually empathetic. Many people have the strength of learning but they are sadly labeled as unmotivated, perpetual students. Some people are disheartened and confused for being too driven when they are focused and strategic. And, I've seen people depressed, anxious, and criticized because they are labeled "push-overs" when in reality, they are servants.

These are examples of people who have been made to feel inadequate and have lost their confidence struggling to be the way others want them to be. Asking them to change the way they live and to use strengths they do not have is like asking them to use their weaker muscles to survive falling off a mountain. I am asking them to strengthen what they have a predisposition for, what they were created with, and to survive that mountain fall differently.

Our instinct to compete, succeed, and belong prods us to take classes and seek advice and help to improve our weaknesses. We won't be made a fool of! We've got to keep the job, the girl, the look! Now, imagine shifting your focus from your weaknesses, even the glaring ones, to developing your strengths.

Learn your strengths and get good at using them. Just because they are strengths doesn't mean they are strong enough. They need to be developed and refined because they all have a down side or "shadow side." For example, the shadow side of being a good communicator is talking too much. The down side of being focused is missing the big picture. Your investment of passion, time, energy, and money into your strengths will grow more than any investment in your weaknesses.

In all probability, our weaknesses will not develop to the same level of competency as our strengths, even after more time and energy and training. But our strengths will improve exponentially. I am a scientist, but my weakness is basic algebra. I took additional courses to improve my algebraic skills. Later, as they began to falter, I took refresher courses.

While adequate, my skills never improved to become my strong point. I will never count on my math skills for my living. When I put the same amount of time into developing my communication, marketing, and psychology skills, they flourished to a level of excellence that I can depend on, and professionally thrive by using. I hire an accountant and statistician who are strong where I am weak. I take the opportunity to do what I do best everyday.

Do you have the opportunity to do what you do best everyday? Chances are you don't. Our natural strength, unfortunately, often goes untapped, either for lack of opportunity or because we don't know what they are. From birth to boardroom, cradle to cubicle, through life and loss, we devote more time remedying our weaknesses than developing and using our strength. Knowing what your strengths are helps but is not essential. You may be using them accidently, out of habit, because you enjoy them, or because you are asked to use them. The strength I encourage you to discover and use for your Sacred Survival shows up naturally and frequently in your life. They are patterns of repeated behavior and result in productivity and satisfaction. They become stronger when they are refined with practice and with understanding.

Until recently, we didn't have the vocabulary to identify and delineate one strength from another. We would say. "She has great people skills." But what does that mean? Does it mean that she is a good listener? Does it mean she is a good talker? It seemed we needed better words to more precisely describe the plethora of strengths in the world. The Clifton Strengths Finder collaborated with The Gallop Organization and Employee Selection Research to identify talents capable of being developed for improved outcomes at work and in school. A measure was established under Clifton to assess respondent's talents. As of 2007, more than two million participants had completed the measure, establishing validity and reliability. This is just one example that underscores a credible process of identifying our abilities that can produce our strength.

Strength can be studied and used in almost every situation. When we experience a desire or longing to do something, and when we learn something quickly and are satisfied, we are probably using our natural abilities. Strengths are an extension of aptitudes and talents that are the building blocks, or raw materials, from which strengths are produced. When our talents are combined with practice, skill, knowledge, and results in near-perfect presentation, we are surviving with our strength. Studies of using strength suggest that their development increases hope, altruism, and self-confidence.

> You will gain far more when developing your strength than you will by trying to improve your weaknesses.

Strength-based survival focuses on the rescue effort, not the cause of the capsizing. Rather than obsessing on the reasons for our circumstances, Sacred Survival moves its attention to the dream, hope, and outcome we are seeking. In psychology, this is what's called solution-focused therapy, developed by Steve De Shazer, Insoo Kim Berg, and their team at the Brief Family Therapy Center in Milwaukee, WI. It concentrates more on the present and future rather than the past. Past experiences are important because they create patterns of behavior and reasoning that is valuable to explore. However, sometimes we get stuck exploring the past to avoid moving into a new future. Sometimes we get stuck in our past because even the painful past that we know is easier to deal with than exploring an unknown future. And sometimes we get stuck in the past because we believe we can fix it. Getting stuck is postponing life. There are many other reasons we have trouble letting go of the past, including not believing we are worth something better or feeling guilty for leaving someone behind. The therapeutic work is more about processing these feelings than it is about unraveling the details of the who, what, where, and why of the past events. Sacred Survival asks, "What about your past was successful? How can that approach be incorporated in the future?"

What makes this approach sacred? When you imagine your survival through the lens of your strengths, you can visualize your future as you and God want it, not as you dread it. From this, you decide what skills and steps are best employed to live out that dream. Spend some time on the vision. Use whatever telescope you have to scrutinize the details of your new dream instead of fixating on the past. The more specific your vision, the more precisely you can create your survival plan. The more time you spend visualizing your future, the more likely you are to see beyond your "basic needs" into your "beautiful wants."

Perhaps your idea of survival is getting by on the basics that you need to sustain your life. Sacred Survival says that you are worthy of more than basic living. You are worthy of spectacular living. It is in the extras that we hear God affirm, "You are valuable." Many practical, frugal people have reminded me that we can't "eat the atmosphere" in an expensive restaurant—the glow of candlelight, the fine damask napkins, and over-the-top service. So why spend good money on it? But some experiences are worth the investment. They tell us that we are worth far more than the basics a drive-through restaurant offers. And this is priceless. Sacredness is in the details.

Looking back might trap you into focusing on what you did wrong if you don't stay present and process your past experiences for your future. Living in the present and going toward the future imagines how to do it differently. Although chronic conditions can be constant and unrelenting, they are also continually changing and will inevitably transform. Consider what changes you want and what part of your past existence you want to keep. Then with this clear vision you can harness your strengths with new confidence to move forward. A sacred survival looks at a life set apart, different, and better than the present. Guided by those successful past moments, you can incorporate those strengths now to achieve another positive outcome.

Essential elements of using our strength are perspective, positivity, and passion. Perspective is the gift of imagination wherein we see opportunities to use our previously proven strengths in new ways for chronic problems. It's not so much that we are improving what we are already good at, as much as it is using what we are good at in places where we are stuck.

Susan was struggling to survive her unemployment and was stuck chasing the type of journalist jobs she had in the past. Her unemployment had outlasted her efforts to network, interview, compete, and all out job-hunt for two years. The situation had become not only chronic, as in long term, but it was a crisis, too. The loss was devastating and tangible. She lost her financial security, housing, private schools, healthcare, and friendships. This led to the intangible losses of confidence, self-esteem, dignity, and hope. When she came to me she had begun to experience anxiety and depression. Counseling began as a way to process her frustration and anger about what went wrong and what she could no longer do. She discussed marriage and divorce and her faltering self-confidence as she prepared for upcoming interviews.

These concerns were important, but it was equally important for her to see that they were distracting her from getting in touch with her true losses. It took some time to get all her words out, not because she hesitated, but because she had so many of them. She, understandably, had a lot of pent-up emotion from years of experiences that she had never confided to anyone. An avalanche of words fell out of her mouth, bursting open the gateway to her heart and soul. Only after she believed she had been heard did she stop talking and begin to listen. She could finally hear me say, "I'm sorry." Before, anything I said was drowned out by the ranting voices in her mind rehearsing the next argument. When she heard me and believed me, she was able to lay down the defenses protecting her from receiving my compassion. Then she was able to pause and consider a new perspective for survival.

> Rather than obsessing on the reasons for your circumstances, Sacred Survival moves its attention to the outcome you are seeking.

The tangible loss she had called financial security was renamed the ambiguous losses of certainty and dignity. The ambiguous loss was much harder to address. Susan knew how to find sources of money in her life. She could apply for a holiday retail job, borrow from her parents, or request aid from the state's system. But she was not prepared to look for her dignity. How could she begin to look for something she didn't know she had lost? Until she named it and acknowledged it, no amount of money would satisfy the loss of her dignity. With dignity, she could live on less money. This didn't mean she could get by the way a young, naïve couple thinks they can live on love. She did need money, but she needed so much more, which she came to understand as dignity. Once she understood the nature of her loss, she could grieve and work through it. She had new energy to climb out of her crisis and gain perspective for a new dream.

Sacred Survival for Susan included gaining awareness of the strengths she possessed. She considered how she used them in the past to feel confident, hopeful, and respected. Her new plan was to find a job that gave value and significance through her strength as a communicator. Did she need to use that talent only as a journalist? No, that was yesterday's dream that she had chased to its death. Her new job search criterion was any world where she could use her strengths. It mattered less what she was communicating and more that she had the opportunity to use her strength of communicating. Satisfaction became valued more than prestige or status. She soon found a sales position that brought her great personal and professional success. She said to me, "I no longer will live with anyone or work anyplace that asks me to live without my strengths."

## STRENGTH BRINGS A PASSION FOR THE FUTURE

Sacred Survival uses strength reasoning because it believes the best in spite of the past. It offers respect and compassion for the "life" lost in the past, and creates a passion for the ongoing survival. Survival is more than instinctual; it is a practice of awareness and thoughtfulness. Thoughts are predictors of happiness because they are attached to what we feel, just like what we feel is attached to what we think. Mental healthcare practitioners practice with the hope that our thoughts can be as important as medication to influence our anxiety and depression. Healthy, passionate, and life-affirming thoughts produce a healthier more passionate and life affirming survival.

Tim had been suffering with back pain for many years and his job required him to sit at a desk, bent over a computer for six hours, which aggravated it more. He was in too much pain to continue working in that position but not in enough pain to file for insurance benefits. His chiropractor and physician both told him that becoming more physical would actually decrease his pain if he became more flexible and lost some weight. It was hard for him to believe when every muscle was screaming, "Rest. Don't move!" Eventually, he left his job because he was too miserable to continue. He wasn't only hurting physically, but his pain was making him irritable and depressed. Initially, his bills went into collection, and his self-worth plummeted. He didn't know how to start a job search because he believed his pain would eliminate him from any job worth having. He didn't know how to cope with unemployment because he felt he was a failure to his family. In essence, he didn't know who he was anymore beyond a victim of pain.

His perspective began to change when his wife expressed how much she valued the way he could adapt to all the demands around the house. Whether it was unpredictable plumbing repairs, last-minute homework crises, or the dozen errands that every household requires, he was flexible and never confused or upset with last-minute change. His wife also appreciated how easily he conversed with the kids' teachers, the church's elders, and the bill collectors. What was difficult for her was easy for him. Tim told her that it came naturally and that he always felt satisfied and fulfilled after he accomplished such tasks. His natural strengths were being able to adapt to frequent change and being able to relate easily to others. He had never identified these abilities as strengths because they came so easily to him. And he had never imagined that they could be used in his professional job search as both a means and end to his livelihood.

Tim and I talked about his pain in the context of his

strength of adaptability. With pain, I explained, you never know what is going to happen. One minute you might feel great, and the next minute you have a burning sensation keeping you in bed. His strength of adaptability enabled him to respond to the demands of the moment even if they changed his plans. He learned to embrace being adaptable, which helped him respond differently to the constant fluctuations in his level of pain. Adaptability became his strong suit that he used to create a different kind of expectation. He could stay positive and productive rather than being battered by change. His strength of relating to others allowed him to trust people and accept some risk in opening up about his pain and suffering. Leaning into these strengths encouraged him to interview and be honest about his assets and abilities. He was also able to return to his friendly Thursday night men's group and contribute to the coffee and pie bill at closing, which helped restore his self-respect.

As he became comfortable with his newly-identified strengths, he sought professional and personal opportunities to use them. He took a job with his brother-in-law at a cleaning service where he became a real asset relating to people and with minute-to-minute changes in work orders. His sense of satisfaction and self-respect reconciled what was inside (his values) with what was outside (his new job). He began to appreciate yesterday for what it taught him about his strengths as an adapter and a relator, and he stopped chasing the past. His passion for living became stronger than his pain. He changed his thoughts from, "I am a failure" to "I know what makes me successful." He focused on the present and the future while honoring the impact of the past.

I worked with a kind woman who felt the loss of close relationships. With more discovery, she identified her ambiguous losses as the loss of companionship, self-esteem, and self-worth. Her strategy had been to become an extrovert and assert herself. She signed up for gatherings requiring her to use social media, Facebook, and email, all of which made her anxious, resentful, and cranky. The world was telling her she had to be outgoing and a networker to have friends. It was like telling a bird that loved to fly that it had to swim in the ocean.

We identified her strengths as being compassionate, serving others, and teaching. She immediately said, "Cross off teaching because I never get to use that." She was a strong teacher, but she was in relationships with people and places where she didn't get to use this strength. By acknowledging and embracing her teaching strength, she began her Sacred Survival. She beamed when she said, "I love teaching." Her Sacred Survival depended on her finding ways to do it. Now she is involved in communities that value teaching. She is discovering the teaching aspect of all her relationships. She teaches her grandchildren how to make mud pies. She teaches her neighbor how to recycle. She writes blogs and articles that teach.

How do her other strengths apply? Clearly this is a compassionate and selfless woman. She gives and gives and gives without asking for anything in return. Perhaps this was her dilemma. I challenged her to heal her rejection by serving herself and showing herself compassionate. In her desire to serve, it didn't occur to her that she needed to take care of herself as much as any other. As she learned how to do this, she filled up with the kind of love that spilled out even more to others.

## ACCEPT RESPONSIBILITY

Sacred Survival believes life is inherently good, not bad. Survival is the normal course of life even as we accept that our physical life on this earth is not without end. Suffering and pain are a distortion of life. It twists the inclination and human predisposition away from progressive development. We are not only created with a built-in striving to live but to make the very best of our existence. Chronic pain and suffering dampen and all but extinguish this desire. Carl Rogers names these natural inclinations as positive regard, including love, recognition, attention, positive self-esteem, self-regard, self-image, and nurturance. When these are absent from our lives, we feel helpless and hopeless.

The pivotal point of Sacred Survival is the awareness that we, as survivors, have to accept responsibility and approach our chronic suffering seeking help and hope. We must surround ourselves with strength encouragers. It is an intentional step taken into a safe and nurturing relationship with God and those around us who demonstrate love, kindness, and a positive regard for us. Rather than focus on what we do not receive, the survivor summons all remaining strength to go after these resources. Sacred Survival starts when we use whatever energy we still have (and there is always some unless life has ceased) to go after the means to live better.

> When you imagine your survival through the lens of your strengths, you can visualize your future as you and God want it, not as you dread it.

## IT'S NOT WHAT'S WRONG, IT'S WHAT'S RIGHT

Many survival strategies focus on the problems that created the suffering. Life becomes a series of questions, such as, "How did I get here?" and "What did I (or everyone else) do wrong?" This perspective uses a language of cynicism, pessimism, and doubt. It diminishes the power of future-thinking and hopeful feeling. Sacred Survival, while not yet a theory, is a belief and practice where the survivor discovers and exploits strengths. It is a lens that views solutions to live with the problem, not necessarily the elimination of the problem. Although this sounds so simple to the point of being discounted by those in pain, its complexity is underestimated given our society's predisposition with problem-solving. We ask what's wrong, which demands we focus on the problem. We get stuck there. In contrast, Sacred Survival invites survivors to implement a "non-problem-solving" framework. The focus becomes about what is right. Some may refer to this as will power. Others call it positive thinking. Sacred Survival suggests that it is more than that. It is being who you are created to be with the radical audacity to believe it will be. "It," however, may not look like what you imagined. Society has various labels that fall in and out of popularity for people who hurt such as codependent, bipolar, or narcissistic. I believe they are real conditions and are really painful. But I encourage you to take your eye off the labels that pigeonhole your existence as a disease or pathology and start survival anew. This will influence the way you see, hear, and listen to your past story and future "happier" ending.

For the professional counselor, this approach may sound like empowering people with therapeutic models, such as solution-focused therapy, narrative therapy, person-centered therapy, and Erickson's life stages, and developmental theories that assert people pass through stages of life (survival) to self-actualization. Survival through use of strengths has a mixture of options to it. It doesn't ask, "What is the outcome I want?" It asks, "What can I do now, using my proven strengths in new ways for a new kind of survival that I have never imagined before?" The connection to spirituality with this approach is the belief that God is beckoning us forward to be who we already are.

Surviving with strength directs us to be responsible for our choices and decisions. It demands a degree of competence for our behavior and survival. We all have the potential to right our path and correct our course of action. However, in today's world of healthy and unhealthy choices, sacred surviving is enhanced when our choices to develop our strengths collaborate with our natural potential to grow, heal, and learn.

The strength approach is a way of thinking and believing. It is rooted in the belief that not only do we have behavioral strengths based on gifts and talents, but our strengths are personal characteristics as well. We survive as we lean into our virtues and values. Sacred Survival rests on the appreciation for our strength. As obvious as that sounds, we have gotten away from sincere appreciation of the positive and overlook the power and beauty of strength. Some survivors expect the world around them to be strong enough, so they don't have to be. Many feel entitled to have others do the heavy lifting, and when they are not available, they sink into the defeating thought pattern, "Why don't I have this?" instead of "Look what I have." That is an understandable reaction to pain, suffering, and a feeling of abandonment or isolation. It is also a sinking ship. It begets more isolation and limits the opportunities to use the very strengths which can create a better existence. It squelches the innate resilience survivors have that is sparked by hope and transformation. Sacred Survival asks what is my life AND what life do I want?

Our strengths are best expressed when they grow out of our connection and respect with God and each other. A translation of the biblical command to "be strong" is to be strengthened, implying that sometimes our strength comes not from within but from another. I can't emphasize enough that our pain and suffering, no matter what kind, need to be acknowledged in the survivor's context and not in comparison to what others are experiencing. Out of this recognition comes the subsequent conversation of strengths that can normalize life and take the crisis out of the chronic problem. By joining with the problem rather than fighting it, we direct our attention toward the solutions. While not minimizing the pain, this perspective can encourage and empower strengths to recognize what can be, and what the potential is.

> God is beckoning us forward to be who we already are.

Above all, sacred strengths create transformation from pessimism to potential. Some survivals make headlines. But this kind of a survival is a small, quiet conversion of change where survival rebounds and doubt diminishes. Survivors must change the way they think about themselves and talk about themselves.

Where does this come from? When you are lost and looking for your destination, you may choose to use the tall store directory in the mall, with all the arrows and colors directing your way. What is the first thing you have to locate? It's the "YOU ARE HERE" spot. Then you can plot out the best route. When you are inputting data on your GPS system, you must enter your starting location, or it can't plot your course. It's not enough to know where you have been. It's not enough to know where you want to go. You must know where you are now. The strength that you possess announces, "You are HERE." That's how we best survive.

Find your strengths. These are the talents God said, "Be faithful with what I have given you and I will give you more."

They will set your course and show you how to take off and land on your Sacred Survival journey. You can go anywhere.

# THOUGHTS TO CONTEMPLATE ABOUT STRENGTH

1. How do we find and take advantage of what we already have?

2. What do you do that comes naturally to you?

3. What do you do that brings you the most satisfaction when you do it?

4. What is the common element in every job you've ever had? (teaching something, nurturing, learning, communicating…)

NOTES:

CHAPTER SIX

# Acceptance

Some of us begin our survival experience by stuffing our pain into a tiny box. After a difficult medical diagnosis or in the aftermath of a trauma like divorce, assault, or abandonment, we shrink the pain monster into a manageable size, shape, or memory. We make it "normal" so we can go on living; we say it's inconsequential and just doesn't matter. That's how we get out of bed in the morning.

## "IT" MATTERS

In Sacred Survival, "it"—the pain of whatever happened to you and whatever has changed the course of your life—does matters. What happened deserves your utmost attention. The pain must escape the box. I want you to consider that your pain is never so immense—like Pandora's Box filled with all the evils of the world—that it can torment you, and never so trivial that you can pretend it doesn't matter.

Everyone's story basically starts the same way. It starts

with being fine. It starts in the "before" part of our survival. We cling to our "before" story and to the memory of when we were fine. We dwell in the good ol' days as if talking about it will somehow bring it back. The fact we are talking about it, though, means there is no going back. We are already living in the "now" and what comes after.

## HOPING AND COPING

Still, we imagine our life will return to, or move toward, what we hope for. We make plans and hope they will get us where we want to go. We hope our plans pan out. We hope that God hears our prayers. We hope we get the life we pray for. But somewhere in between what we hope for and what we live with lies the challenge to accept what is real. In that space, we readjust our outlook and rewrite our story with a new ending. How the story unfolds depends on our survival strategy and coping mechanisms.

We use many coping mechanisms as strategies and practices to survive. Some have the potential to make our survival a little more sacred like the practice of developing our strength. We learn coping mechanisms by watching others and trying them out for ourselves. Some work. Others don't. Sometimes they become comfortable routines or habits deterring us from trying new and better ways of coping with life. Then, no matter if they help or hurt us, we remain stuck in a pattern, repeating the way we approach survival, expecting change even if it is unlikely.

Whether we have a debilitating physical illness or a complicated emotional problem, each situation creates unique demands. Along with those demands are complex reasons explaining why our coping mechanisms for chronic suffering don't work. One explanation is that we get stuck inside the problem, unable to see another way of living or viewing it. This is understandable. So much of survival depends on staying fixed in the midst of the problem and reacting minute by minute to the demands of staying alive. We get stuck in our frenzied mantras: "Just keep on trying." "Don't give up." "One more time!" We don't have time to learn a new stroke when we are frantically doing the dog paddle to keep afloat. But this may keep us from seeing the bigger picture. Without a broader perspective, we may never believe a different way is possible.

> Somewhere in between what we hope for and what we live with lies the challenge to accept what is real.

Learning the practice of sacred acceptance is to learn how to accept what is, while not giving up on what can still be. It shifts helplessness to hopefulness because it trusts that we are worth everything, but doesn't expect that we are able to control anything. When we practice sacred acceptance, we don't stop hoping for the best, though our survival isn't tied to getting it. Hope is good. But hope can become a merciless master if it drives our happiness instead of directing our vision. When hope is only a mirage of relief, we don't know what is or isn't acceptable. The practice of acceptance merges hope with truth. That is where redemption and rescue are born.

## THE SACRED STRATEGY OF ACCEPTANCE

This chapter asks you to consider using acceptance in a new way. Perhaps you are already familiar with this practice, and this chapter will give you additional ways to use acceptance in your survival. Perhaps you have heard of this practice but have rejected it thinking that acceptance isn't a real strategy, just more about doing nothing. I assure you, it is a powerful, though often difficult, coping principle to practice. It is based on your perception of the situation you are enduring. Your attitude about problems makes a significant difference in your survival.

As a professional counselor, a friend, and a pastor I have acquired both scientific research and anecdotal accounts pointing to one's attitude as a significant predictor of life satisfaction. A healthy perception of your situation can increase overall well-being and restore the conviction that your circumstances are survivable. Important survival tasks include becoming aware, incorporating your strengths, and practicing how you perceive your life in order to evaluate what you can change, versus what you can accept. This process, like no other, can lessen depression and anxiety related to the losses you have experienced when your life detoured.

Acceptance is the second practice in Sacred Survival. What sets it apart from other acceptance theories is that it doesn't ask you to accept your condition or situation that threatens you. But it doesn't ask you to change what you cannot change, either. It asks you to accept the truth of how you are coping with your situation. It asks you to accept that you have important thoughts and feelings about your circumstances that shouldn't be buried or denied. Sacred acceptance is facing the truth about how you have survived up till now, for better or worse. And, now you can accept that there is a new way to survive. The new way can put you in touch with your pain, which is uncomfortable or scary. But only when you become aware of your pain and accept that it is real, will you begin to take care of it. Your pain says, "What you have been through is real and worth caring about." Without accepting your true painful thoughts and feelings you are distracted with superficial thoughts and feelings and react with solutions that miss the mark. This kind of acceptance is risky but has great benefits. It is a little threatening but will ultimately protect you.

Sacred acceptance asks you to be curious, humble, and brave enough to lay down the weapons you've been using to protect and distract yourself and accept the truth about the way you've been surviving versus how you can survive better.

## THE DOWNSIDE OF HOPE

Acceptance begins when we understand what we can and cannot control and where our control comes from. What we depend on has a certain amount of control over our life. Unfortunately, we try to control the very things that we can't and discount what we can. For better or worse, we resist accepting the hardship in our life, hoping that it will go away. We hope that given enough time, money, help, strength, or miracles we will have power over what we currently cannot change. Hope is one of the things that keeps us alive, but a sacred survival knows what to accept, what to hope for, and how to combine them for the best possible life. Asking someone to give up hope can be cruel and dangerous. But hope in our private version of happiness can keep us stuck, rotating, spinning, and whirling in place without change. That kind of hope undermines healthy acceptance and postpones our life until we are barely alive. What does it take to shift from hoping for the life you used to have to accepting the life that you still can have?

Our society teaches the art of negotiation. When we negotiate our acceptance of pain and suffering, it becomes a process of giving up more and more to live with less and less. We give up ground and become willing to accept less than we ever thought we would. This is not a Sacred Survival. This is just losing ground.

## THE BEGINNING OF ACCEPTANCE

Where does your hope come from? Is it based on external or internal forces? This awareness and understanding moves you to practices of letting go, going on, and accepting and receiving help. The wisdom is in knowing what to accept and what to hope for.

Survival isn't just about asking, hoping, and praying for what we want. Survival is about acknowledging and accepting what is. Why is acceptance so important? In my research and practice, I have found that those who practiced sacred acceptance had less depression and anxiety. And when they had less depression and anxiety, they experienced fewer difficulties related to their chronic situation.

When I was first taught the concept of acceptance, it infuriated me. I thought, "How dare you tell me to accept my chronic condition, this thorn in my side. I will never surrender!" Everyone always told me, "You're a fighter. Never give up!" It took me years of prayer and practice to learn that sacred acceptance isn't giving up. It isn't settling for less. It is moving towards a new, meaningful life. It is the belief that even if I cannot control this condition, it will not control me. It is a life that saves the energy spent struggling for what was lost and reinvests it in what is and what will be.

I have counseled people who have given an all-consuming amount of energy trying to change and control life. They spend so much desperate or angry energy struggling to return to the life they once had, that there is very little left to experience their present life or move toward a new life. There are people who are utterly defined by their illnesses, or their poverty, or their past divorces that they have lost the person that God created them to be. I've learned how to help people dream a new dream and pursue changes that improve their lives at the same time. It's not an either-or proposition. What matters is that we live with our suffering and become more than our misery.

## LET GO OF OLD STRATEGIES

Sacred acceptance lets go of old ineffective strategies. This takes help. When we survive with sacred practices, we don't have to go toe-to-toe with the dark force of suffering alone. We are in community with those who hold sacred space for us and carry some of the pain. We have help, and that is helpful in itself. I have heard countless songs, sermons, and poems that encourage us to lay our heavy burdens down. Laying our burden down is the beginning of acceptance. It does not mean that we give up. It means we accept that we cannot control everything.

I remember when I helped move my mom into a new apartment. I was carrying a couple of heavy boxes until my head and shoulders ached. I knew I had to set them down, but I worried that no one would pick them up. I worried that they might be forgotten or not handled the way I wanted. When I eventually I set them down, I worried, "Why wasn't anyone picking them up?" I obsessed about the contents and these boxes. I spent so much time worrying and trying to control where these boxes would go that I didn't get any relief from setting them down. I still clenched my shoulders, furrowed my brow, and bent over to keep an eye on the boxes. I thought I had laid my burden down—but I really hadn't. I had only laid it down physically. Mentally and emotionally I was still carrying it. I hadn't accepted my role in the process. The boxes were in

> Learning the practice of sacred acceptance is to learn how to accept what is, while not giving up on what can still be.

control of me. Acceptance is the practice of knowing that you can't control your circumstances, but neither will they control you. In Sacred Survival, God is holding our burden. Lay it down and feel the relief.

One of the great paradoxes in survival is that, on one hand, it encourages us to speak up and boldly go after what we think we need for life; on the other hand, survival demands quiet patience, courage, and acceptance of what cannot be changed. We don't always get to choose if we survive, but we can choose how we survive. Choose acceptance—the kind that says, "I will accept what I cannot change." I will lay down the fight against myself and pick up with my strengths to go forward.

## CALL IT BY NAME

True acceptance recognizes what we are fighting, losing, and accepting. When we call our adversary by name, we begin to take away its power because we take away some of its mystery. When it is in plain sight, it becomes something we can face, think about, and deal with, rather than run from or fight. Our adversary—illness, unemployment, or someone abusive—created a loss that now threatens our happiness. When we acknowledge what was taken, we make it real and integrate it into our lives where healing can begin. We can't incorporate what is imaginary. Name it, see it, and then decide what needs to be accepted.

I start a new survival journey every day focusing on what I can and cannot control. (There's very little I can control!) With that perspective I begin to accept what is the best for my life, each and every separate day. Today's best looks different from yesterday and may look all together different tomorrow. But it is always about accepting who I believe God created me to be this day, in this moment. I've stopped chasing yesterday where depression lives. And I've stopped waiting for tomorrow where uncertainty and anxiety abound. I've stopped asking why my life is the way it is and focused on what my life is. Sometimes the "why" doesn't matter. I may never know the reasons for my pain or completely understand it, but in Sacred Survival, I still find a greater place of order in my uncertainty than in the supposed certainty of false control.

## TELL ME EXACTLY WHAT IT IS

Sometimes we reject acceptance because it's a difficult concept to understand and often not explained well. When Parkinson's disease attacked Jacob's body, he lost more than his career as a firefighter. He lost his identity. Jacob's survival depended not on accepting his unfair physical condition, but on accepting that he was having painful thoughts and feelings about his diagnosis. His thoughts and feelings were attacking him with doubts and depression. If he concentrated only on his diagnosis, he would be ignoring the impact that his emotions were making. But he didn't want to accept that he was depressed. He wanted to put all his energy into fighting his diagnosis and finding a new profession. I didn't want him to give up pursuing the best physical improvement he could get. But I wanted him to accept that he was depressed so he could treat his depression and take care of himself. If he got the best medical care and found a new career but never treated the depression associated with losing his dream to be a firefighter, his long-term survival would be threatened with a vague longing for that which had never been identified. Naming his loss was the key to uncovering his painful thoughts and feelings. Facing them was the beginning of accepting them as the real culprit that needed his care and attention. When he took care of himself this way, he could go on to a better and stronger survival, capable of creating a new dream.

For Jacob, the word *acceptance* had been attached to the idea of giving up hope and resigning himself to a life he didn't want. He saw it as the end of something rather than the dynamic process of moving from one place to another. Whenever he heard me use the word acceptance, he could only hear, "Just accept it. There's nothing left to do now." As Jacob and I talked about his life-changing crisis, we began to reframe the idea of acceptance. Eventually, he realized that it was about what he had to accept—not just the physical nature of his condition but his emotional response to the disease. He couldn't change the fact that he had Parkinson's. But now that he accepted he was having a hard time coping with it, he could begin to cope differently. Then the Parkinson's wouldn't be in control of him. He understood it as, "I can't control this disease, but it doesn't need to control me." Instead of, "There's nothing left to do now," we rephrased it as "Now what?" which better expresses its innate hope and promise of a beautiful future.

## WHAT ARE WE ACCEPTING?

Changing the way we think about our circumstances can change how we feel and behave. Cognitive behavioral therapy suggests that we can replace erroneous, negative feelings with more realistic and positive patterns of thought and that our feelings will follow in that positive pathway. Cognitive behavioral therapy is effective in many situations, but it's not the only path to healing. Sometimes the thoughts aren't faulty. Jacob's thought, "This diagnosis isn't fair," was accurate. Trying to change it to something like, "It could be worse," would be a waste of time. Accepting his thoughts as true, along with accepting that they made him sad and anxious, was the beginning of getting the care he needed. It's like treating a bronchial infection. If you don't know what you're really treating, you continue to feel lousy. You can deny you have bronchitis and try to change it into a simple cold, but until you accept it, you won't take the correct antibiotics. I believe it is important to acknowledge and clarify your thoughts and related feelings, accept that they are real, and treat them instead of ignoring them.

Over time, Jacob learned how to let his thoughts and feelings come and go without fighting them. When he accepted them instead of denying them, he could plan a course of action that would care for his pain and prepare him to change for the better. Acceptance as a Sacred Survival practice doesn't ask that he accept having Parkinson's. It doesn't ask that he accept a life of less value in the world or that life is unfair. Acceptance as a Sacred Survival practice asks that Jacob (and you) accept that the thoughts and feelings are really happening rather than denying them. What do you accept and what do you change? You accept that, based on your true thoughts and feelings, you have options for a better way to react and survive. You can change your reaction from unhealthy to healthy and from ineffective to effective. When Jacob accepted that he was feeling sad and useless, he addressed those feelings directly. Eventually, knowing what he lost and what he longed for led him to become a caring, nurturing counselor, helping rescue people from all kinds of hot messes.

Here's another example. You might be feeling angry around your boss. What thoughts stirred up those feelings? Clarifying the thoughts mixed in with those feelings may reveal you feel hurt and rejected by the way he treats you in front of coworkers, not angry. When you accept that you have those feelings, you can pay attention to how you react to them. Do you get anxious? Do you push them away with work, do you drink, or do you withdraw? Once you accept your pattern of reactions instead of denying them, you can consider what other options you have. Before, you might have reacted by yelling, quitting your job, and getting drunk—all motivated by anger. But your anger was just a cover-up for hurt. When you accept that you were feeling hurt, rejected, and lonely you can react differently. Now you can ask, what will soothe my hurt instead of calm my anger? Your new reaction will treat the true pain, and in that truth there is a more Sacred Survival. To be clear, you didn't accept the way your boss treated you. You didn't accept the initial feelings of anger. You searched out your true thoughts and feelings and chose to accept that they were real—so that you could really respond to what you had lost.

Every time I practice acceptance, I am surprised that it requires so many steps and so much effort before I get to where I need to be. There are no shortcuts. When I think I have it figured out, I probably don't. Just yesterday I was reminded that I shouldn't try to take shortcuts in the process. I got a message telling me that I was turned down for a medical trial. When I received the email, I was in the car with my husband running the errands of a typical Saturday. In that moving car, buckled in by a seatbelt, I was not able to get my mind around what just happened and its implications. My husband asked me if I was disappointed. I told him that I was trying to look at the "bright side" of this decision. It would free up my time and take a little stress off me. But I remained quiet, churning, unable to express my thoughts or feelings. In that moment I wanted to criticize those "ill-advised, irresponsible, and silly people" who made the decision to eliminate me from the study. I wanted to lash out and condemn the doctors, hospital, and the entire healthcare system in America—no, the whole world! We went to lunch and I ate a lot of french fries.

Later that night, when it was quiet in my room and quiet in my head, I practiced accepting this news with the elements of sacred space, place, and silence. I needed to calm the chaos within my struggle. I needed help with my painful thoughts and feelings. I began by studying my thoughts, then becoming aware of them, and observing my reaction to them. My first thought was that the doctors in charge of this are making a huge mistake. When I went a little deeper, I accepted my true feelings that were a little scarier and tempting to ignore: "How could they reject me and take away my hope?"

> The practice of acceptance merges hope with truth. That is where redemption and rescue are born.

In the car my feelings seemed to be arrogance and anger. When I accepted my true thoughts of rejection and abandonment, I understood that my true feelings were hurt and fear. Moving from anger to hurt and from arrogance to fear was critical to my letting go and going on with my Sacred Survival. My initial surface thoughts and feelings would have resulted in a destructive behavior. I would have criticized my doctors and probably alienated them. I might have cancelled future appointments and abandoned all of my treatments. My initial feelings were superficial. I tried to stuff them down with french fries.

When I discovered my true thoughts and feelings, I could accept them because they were clear, and they rang true. It's easier to accept something when you're not arguing about its truth and reality. I was hurt and wanted to lash out or hide from the people who rejected me. My options included running from the rejection or healing the hurt of rejection. Healing required seeking out ways to be included, accepted, and validated. I wanted to be worth people's investment. Where do I get that sense of worth? Not by being angry and running away. I would more likely find it by running toward sources of support and understanding. I reached out to my best friend, sister, and God, all whom I could count on for comfort and acceptance. Whew! What a different journey. What a different outcome.

There are many valid ways of coping with emotional and physical pain including pharmaceutical medication, talk therapy, physical activity, and mindfulness. The beginning of any helpful coping strategy is to better assess what your painful condition has taken from you and then consider how to live differently without it. Sometimes you initially feel worse when you accept your true thoughts and feelings of fear and hurt. Not everyone can handle it. But with help you can handle that things aren't what they used to be. Your whole world will be transformed when you stop battling to control the incontrollable. You realize that the ground beneath you is shifting. Things are uncertain, and there's no turning back. The world around you is different now—unrecognizable— and there's nothing you do about it. The future is staring you in face, and you're not sure if you like it. You don't have to like it. When you admit that, you can ask, now what?

In this light, survival that is sacred focuses more on what is happening while still hoping for improvement. It is a loving, accepting response instead of an angry, hateful battle where you are both the victim and the bully, neither of which is nice to live with.

## ACCEPTANCE LIVES IN THE PRESENT

Acceptance is a dynamic process. It is not over and done in one day. Often it's a difficult daily practice, because we live so passionately in the past and the future. A helpful practice I've developed is a way to get grounded to the present. I ask people to notice all five of their senses. I invite them to imagine walking outside to the car and become aware of the sounds. What do you hear? Do you hear leaves crunching under your feet, traffic in the distance, children playing, birds chirping, or the lawn equipment buzzing? What do you smell? Do you smell freshly cut grass, the exhaust of a car, or your own cologne or perfume? What do you feel? Do you feel the crunch of gravel, the scratchy wool coat, or a soft scarf around your neck? What do you see? What do you taste? Here is the point of this practice: when you are aware of your senses, you can't help but be present. When you are present, you can notice your feelings and reactions to your feelings.

## WHERE DOES ACCEPTANCE COME FROM?

Your beliefs about your chronic pain, physical or emotional, play a central role in how you survive long-term. Who or what you believe controls your pain will have one of the greatest impacts on both physical and emotional functioning. Do you think external factors, like your medical support, relationships, food, exercise, and the weather control your future? Or do you believe that God alone controls your life moment by moment? Believing that outside forces have the greatest impact on your condition causes you to rely on external factors. This is known as having an external locus of control. In contrast, an internal locus of control places responsibility for the course of your condition and circumstances on internal forces. It asserts that your attitude, personal drive, sense of responsibility, personality, and individual pursuits and instincts most impact your condition. Your beliefs about where your control comes from affects how satisfied you are with the quality of your life, partly because of the control you feel, and partly because it may help you accept what you cannot control.

The philosophy surrounding the locus of control is woven into all aspects of life. Kevin, who was able to get a job after many months of unemployment, believed that the economy was finally picking up and that his uncle helped him get the job. He has an external locus of control. Ann, who was recently employed, believed that her strong work ethic, perseverance, and efforts in continuing education helped her get the job. She has an internal locus of control. Neither one is right or wrong. But it is helpful to know where you think your control comes from.

We even have a specific health locus of control, where we believe our health status is affected. There is evidence that supports the benefits and risks of operating from both an external and an internal locus of control as related to our health. Some evidence suggests an external control is associated with greater sadness, and less motivation to take care of oneself physically. It is associated with avoidance and escape coping strategies, greater pain, and lower general self worth. It suggests that when we rely on others to help our situation, we may not be as motivated and disciplined in our physical survival. Accepting personal responsibility for life's outcomes, which is an internal control system, is connected to less anxiety and depression. It seems that our beliefs about the healthcare treatment will affect the success of the treatment. But it is not as cut-and-dry as that.

Acceptance is not resignation and giving up. It's saying, "Okay, this is part of my life. Now what?" It is the belief that even if I cannot control this condition, it will not control me.

I can't predict the outcome of my clients' chronic conditions, but I can help create beneficial and effective behaviors based on what they think they can control. For some, believing in themselves becomes a powerful preventative measure, motivating them to be mindful, exercise, or adopt good diets. Their internal control describes the belief that control of future outcomes exists primarily within oneself, even if it is God who stirs them to be their best. External control describes the belief that outside forces such as people, employers, doctors, or chance most likely control what will happen in one's life.

Because I am the type who likes to be in control, I've survived with an internal system of control when it came to taking care of my health condition. This isn't just because I am a control freak; it is because I believe in taking responsibility for my care. That quality made psychological interventions effective for me. Taking personal responsibility is one of the core requirements of emotional therapy. I was motivated to control my chronic illness through personal activities and relationships necessary to maintain my health status. But when I was more honest, I came to accept that I am afraid of depending on others for my survival and tend to react by pushing others away. I disguised this fear with labels of accountability, strength, and conscientiousness. When I accepted the true thoughts and feelings about my health care, I could look at other ways of responding to the challenges of living with a chronic illness. I began to survive by addressing the fear instead of hiding behind false bravado.

For someone dealing with a short-term situation like a broken leg, self-reliance is mostly effective. But in the course of chronic, uncontrollable diseases and circumstances that are unlikely to resolve, an internal system of control may prevent us from taking advantage of the help all around. I have seen people with long-term illness gradually move from stubbornly (and arrogantly) relying on themselves to accepting help from others when their crisis was redefined as chronic. With that acceptance, they could redefine getting help from feeling helpless to feeling hopeful as others were accepted into their life. As much as I love to be in control, and as good as it feels to rely on myself, depending on forces outside of ourselves may be advantageous if we struggle with chronic illness and pain.

What do you do with these contrasting thoughts about operating from an internal versus external control? Is one way better than the other? Sacred Survival seeks to uncover where your think your control comes from and connect that awareness with acceptance. It asks, "Where does control come from? What do I control? What am I letting control me?" In the ever-increasing world that integrates physical, emotional, and spiritual practices, I challenge you to think about who you depend on, and how you attempt to control your life.

This can make the difference in holding on and letting go, and letting go and going on. It is beautifully described in the sacred prayer: "Lord help me accept what I cannot change, give me the courage to change what I can, and the wisdom to know the difference."

## ACCEPTANCE ISN'T CONTROL

The coping mechanism of acceptance is a willingness to experience a chronic condition (emotional and physical) without trying to control it. There are numerous undesired experiences in our life that cannot be controlled or prevented. Acceptance is acknowledging this reality by the choices we make and actions we take.

Coping mechanisms fostering the acceptance of chronic problems challenge the goal of curing the chronic condition.

Our past efforts at surviving reflect how we tried to control or eliminate our problem, which might have actually been detrimental rather than beneficial. Let's face it, we can't eliminate some people from our life much as we would like to. But we can accept that they stir up thoughts and feelings, which when accepted, we can respond to differently. Spending all our energy trying to eliminate our boss from our life is better spent accepting that he's in our life driving us crazy, and it's time to consider different options of living with him.

My work has led me to expand my study of coping with chronic problems to include accepting responses. Acceptance of chronic problems and unfortunate events does not require understanding them. If we are resilient, we probably possess the belief that good and bad life events happen, and understanding is not a necessary component of healthy adaptation. After interviewing dozens of clients with chronic problems, I discovered that those not persistent in finding perfect solutions to them but who accept the existence of them, without giving up hope of improvement, live better.

Acceptance is not the automatic coping choice for us. Most people with chronic problems understandably live with the hope that their circumstances will be cured. If you are unemployed, you want to believe that you will be offered the new job. If you are financially bankrupt, perhaps what gets you through is avoiding the realities of changing your life style and believing your ship is about to come in. If you are divorced or widowed, you may not want to accept your new single status and be praying for a new relationship.

Hoping for change is a powerful force. But it has gone powerfully wrong when you become obsessed with making your problem and its pain go away. Then, it may be time to try additional strategies to survive these circumstances. How we respond to those choices will influence our next choices.

I believe that when we make higher functioning choices, we will live better with chronic problems than when we merely try to eliminate them or avoid them.

Likewise, people who avoid facing their problems tend to make lower functioning choices. Accept that we will continually encounter problems as a prerequisite for coping with life. I cannot stress enough that this kind of acceptance is not resignation and giving up. It's saying, "Okay, this is part of my life. Now what?" Chronic problems have the potential to alter a life to such a degree that we lose our identity and how we function. Identifying all that we lost allows us to begin reconstructing a better survival, because we realize what we want to replace, or we accept that we have to live without it. Either way, the recognition of the loss will stir up true feelings that have to be faced and dealt with so we can finally move on. That's the kind of truth that will set us free from our pain. I start every day with this practice. It gets easier and easier, and we become better and better at this practice when we surround ourselves with reminders that life really is meant to be beautiful, not just bearable.

If I you think I am proposing that you accept the circumstances in your life that have created a life filled with loss, or that you accept your painful thoughts and feelings, let me be very clear: the only thing I suggest you accept is that they are currently occurring in your life. They are not tied to your worth or value as a human being. You do not deserve to suffer. So don't push the thoughts and feelings away. Accept them, but only for as long as it takes to know what is real and what is not. Accepting your scary thoughts and feelings isn't to keep them but to transform them. Facing them means you can do something with them. It is to accept what you can change and what you cannot, and then let go of what holds you back and go on to what transforms you to a life you love.

## THOUGHTS TO CONTEMPLATE ABOUT ACCEPTANCE

1. What is the difference between your thoughts and your feelings?

2. What kind of thoughts are the most difficult for you to accept? What emotions do they stir up? How do you react when you feel those feelings? What are some other ways of reacting?

3. How do you get grounded to the present and stop thinking about the past and future? Take a moment to write down what you hear, see, feel, taste, and smell. After you are finished, describe how this practice prevented you from thinking about the past or future.

NOTES:

CHAPTER 7

# Compassion

## COMPASSION UNITES

Let me begin this chapter with a reference found near the end of the Bible:

"Behold, the dwelling place of God is with man. He will dwell with them, and they will be his people, and God himself will be with them as their God. He will wipe away every tear from their eyes, and death shall be no more, neither shall there be mourning nor crying nor pain anymore, for the former things have passed away…And He said, Behold, I am making all things new" (Revelation 21:3–5).

God created everything anew in Genesis, and He ends with the promise to do the same again. All things can be made new when God dwells *with* us, and when we are renewed with compassion. This invites you to consider that the practice of compassion renews you to go on to a Sacred Survival.

As humans, we are created to feel unique and crave healthy attention that declares, "You are special!" But in our global world, we have become closer physically, and emotionally more distant. We know more and more, about more and more, until we have too much to remember about anything. With each new piece of data, we are forced to decide consciously and subconsciously how to store it on our "brain-disk." If we are created for relationships, and we are, then what will create relationships and enrich them? We create and enrich relationships when we find ourselves inside the experience of another and when we find another's life inside our own. Compassion doesn't just help us relate to each other—it unites us.

## COMPASSION FOR PAIN

I appreciate the psalms in the Bible because they tell of another survival story. King David was a real survivor and I think it was partly because he understood compassion. He cried out again and again for the compassion of God. "I will call out to you in the day of my trouble. You, oh Lord, are a compassionate and gracious God" (Psalm 86:7,15). Sacred Survival is grounded in compassion. Without it, we may be reluctant to practice the acceptance of our strengths, thoughts, and feelings because we do not want to experience any suffering. We may try to be tough and independent, or weak and helpless, unable to find ourselves in the heart of God or find God in our heart of suffering. Without compassion, relationships are infantile, exits are ugly and done badly, and decisions lack the heart-felt element that will sustain them when our mind says, "Stop!" Compassion is the voice of truth that understands our needs and directs our path into healing and strength. Without the practice of compassion, pain is intolerable.

## SURPRISED BY PAIN?

The Bible includes many references to pain. And yet we are uncomfortable, even surprised, when we discover it in our own life. I understand being angry or sad, but surprised? Maybe, as Americans in this day and age, we think we are entitled to less pain. We have better educations, better houses, and a longer physical existence than our parents. But there is no precedent in history of a life without sorrow, pain, and illness. While the Bible records many examples of healings, it also mentions growing feeble, failing eyesight, and painful illness. Through hundreds of years of slavery, God's people suffered great pain and loss. Moses was slow of speech; Paul lived with a "thorn" in his flesh. Yet we prefer to focus on the healings. Of course we do.

I have chosen to focus in my profession on the suffering and pain in our lives. Not the "why" of it, but the hopeful "what now?" of it. It's too prevalent to ignore. In America, more than 60% of our population has at least one chronic illness and many of them painful. Some have survived heart attacks, cancer, and sports injuries. If you are healthy or young, chances are you are taking care of someone who is not. More than half of marriages end in divorce. Bankruptcy filings are rising. Violence among our youth is at an all time high. Either you have suffered, are suffering, or will suffer at some point in your life. That's a lot of suffering! Most of us are surviving something that either threatens us, our family, or a friend. Even if the threat is over, we are still battling its aftermath. Like the aftershocks of an earthquake, it is equally terrifying.

This kind of suffering begs for the practice of sacred com-

> Of one thing I am sure, this practice of compassion begins with letting go of our fears.

passion. Ordinary compassion believes in and practices empathy but grows weary when the situation or suffering lingers. Compassion that lacks a sacred practice tries to control the process of grief by directing how the suffering should decrease or the sufferers should "get over" their problem. It tries to fix and have power over another. It tries to lead where it thinks is best rather than follow where the suffering goes. Compassion becomes sacred when it holds sacred space for another's pain to such an extent that words do not try to fix the suffering but suffers with them so they are not alone. It is sacred when it renews other's strength so that they can let go of their pain and go on to their gain. It is sacred when it lives in the life of the one suffering rather than trying to redefine it and fit it into what is reasonable for us.

Where does this kind of compassion come from? Does it emerge naturally, or is it learned—and how? What moves one person to feel compassionate and another to appear insensitive, even hardhearted? Is compassion something for desperate times, or can it be a constant presence and way of life?

Of one thing I am sure: this practice of compassion begins with letting go of our fears. This will uncover our deepest and scariest feelings of shock and confusion in response to the overwhelming thought, what if this happened to me? Or worse, I can't believe this is happening to me. This kind of fear absorbs so much of our feeling capacity that there is very little space in our hearts saved for a deeply compassionate love. This kind of fear forces us away from the one needing compassion, even if we are the ones aching to receive it. Pain is such a selfish and indomitable bully that it closes our minds and hearts to feeling anything else. When we experience our own physical or emotional pain, it can consume our mental and emotional energy so that compassion is driven out or not even considered.

Sacred compassion is guided and provided by God and His Spirit. This means that we don't have to completely know what we are doing. We worship and follow God without always having a step-by-step plan. We do so as extensions of God's living Spirit in us and around us. Sometimes we don't even know we are being compassionate, but we are. Remember those whom Jesus commended in Matthew 25 for feeding the hungry and giving drink to the thirsty. They had to ask, "When?" They may not have even known that they were acting compassionately. They acted out of morality and as conduits of God. Imagine what you could do if you did so consciously, intentionally, and as a way of life.

## EMPATHIZING OR CONDONING?

The word *compassion* has both emotional and intellectual foundations. The etymology of "compassion" is Latin, meaning "co-suffering." It is more than empathy. It wants to alleviate another's suffering. I like this definition more than the more commonly stated "suffering *with* another." Both are true but imply different participation. Imagine being in an airplane. If I am with the flight crew, I might be standing by. If I am the co-pilot, I am engaged and helping. Although it is not my plane to fly, I have some sense of duty.

Perhaps this is why people shy away from being compassionate. It is daunting to be inside another's life. When I interviewed people about their thoughts on compassion, I found they often confused having empathy with condoning another's life situation. There is this American fear that if we empathize and stay in another's suffering, we are saying that we accept their situation or that we will fix it. Our sense of morality, real or make-believe, says that we should turn our backs on the kind of suffering that we judge as being "their fault" or that is the result of behavior we believe is wrong. We think that giving compassion lets the other "off the hook."

I think that's why our compassion can wane for those suffering from addiction or abuse. We lose compassion for the addicts who have continual relapses. Even the addicts lose compassion for themselves. After repeated relapse, people become hardened to their suffering, thinking that they should have more willpower and overcome their problems. Standers-by attempt to apply tough love thinking, "Well, compassion didn't help, so maybe a little tough love will. That will show them! Then they'll change." It is a careful practice to be in another's recurring and ugly suffering. But hear me: compassion does not mean we are condoning the situation. It means we are suffering along with them and holding the pain that perpetuates their trouble.

The problem isn't the act of compassion; it is that we expect the wrong outcome from it. We think the goal of compassion is to relieve another's pain. We think comfort is the endgame and stop when people feel better. Compassion is the gate opener, but it is only the beginning. It provides the space for people to become aware of their thoughts and feelings so that they have the freedom to choose new options, as we discussed in the chapter on acceptance. But without compassion, those hurting are left to the only devices they know: defensiveness and withdrawal. Their healing work starts after we give compassion. Unfortunately, they linger in the place of compassion instead of rising up to begin again. Although that might be a warm protective place, there is little chance of change if the survival work stops there. Think of compassion as a kind of serum that rejuvenates and jump-starts their lives.

Imagine thinking, "I should get some exercise. I should take better care of myself physically. I'm not sure how out of shape I am and I'm too afraid to find out. Now I'm depressed. Maybe I'll just stay home and order pizza. Besides, if I talk to my sister about this one more time, she's just going to roll her eyes." Then you hear a voice of compassion on the TV. It's Jenny, no, it's Marie or Dan Marino. They know your pain. They get you! In that moment of compassion, you feel better. You even make the phone call to sign up for their weight-loss program. You pay the money, get on the scale, take your measurements, and buy cute gym clothes. You feel GREAT. You feel understood because someone recognized your suffering. What relief.

Then you stop. You don't go to the meeting, or to the gym, or to the produce aisle at the Piggly Wiggly. After receiving a little compassion, the pain that had been pushing you to do something has dissipated enough for you to slip back into old habits. There, you repeat the cycle of suffering where your friends and family have grown tired and desensitized. Only the paid celebrities stick with you.

See how that worked, or, rather, didn't work? The compassion you were given gave you a burst of energy and life force. But that's where our survival can get jammed. We think that compassion is the fix because it feels good. But it's only the beginning of change. It creates the momentum for the real survival effort. The compassion we feel or give is like a pain-killer for someone recovering from surgery. The relief you get from the analgesic sets you up for the hard work of physical therapy and recovery.

## GOD'S COMPASSION IS REAL

When I suggest you will feel better and live better with compassion, that may sound like some cliché to tuck away with the other positive self-help platitudes. This may sound like more empty words that are supposed to make us feel better, lessen our pain, and make up for all that we've lost. I don't want you to come and go with words of encouragement today that are easily forgotten because they don't land in your heart and soul.

What do you need when you are sick or dying? You need compassion. It may not feel like enough when you're filled with pain and the loss of what it stole from you. But compassion will change the course of your survival if applied well. We often think we only have to practice what we do, but it is equally important to learn how to properly receive. (And, in receiving, we are more able to give.) This is the case of compassion. It sounds too simple to be life-changing. It's a lot like telling people that they need to breathe. Why do we have to remind people to do something that should be automatic? Breathing, like compassion, is not always automatically chosen. When we're afraid and in pain we hold our breath. We need to be reminded again and again to breathe when our bodies abandon us in the presence of pain and suffering. Why don't we appreciate the simple things that can change us the most? We've come to put our faith in sophisticated technology, medications, and something new to try. But practicing compassion is just like taking deep breaths—and we have to be reminded of its power through encouragement, testimonies, and experience.

> We expect the wrong outcome from compassion. We think comfort is the endgame and stop when people feel better. That's only the beginning.

The book of Psalms is my favorite book in the Bible, probably because it's filled with testimony of David calling out to God. David is my champion for physical and emotional breakdowns. "Oh God, Oh God, I cry out to you in pain."

He doesn't deny his pain. He doesn't pretend to be invincible or impervious to pain and the threat of death. He isn't too spiritual or too holy to say, "HELP! I need you." This is where our help begins. We begin to heal when we cry out about our loss, whatever we've lost. In our crying out, we begin to feel better as we are met with compassion.

Imagine a little boy running through the day with a cut on his elbow or a sprained wrist. He doesn't tell you he's hurt so you don't have the opportunity to apply a bandage and relieve his pain. If God knows our pain, why do we have to cry out and tell him? Because until we stop and open up our lives up to Him, we miss His cure. Parents can run behind their bleeding child with the Band-Aid, knowing what he needs. But if the child doesn't stop, seek his parents and stretch out his wounded arm, he misses the cure.

Compassion might be tangible from God, or through a neighbor, or in medical solutions. Compassion can also be present in a very real but mystical presence of our spirituality. There's a reason we feel better when we are in the presence of a loved one and don't have to go it alone. We were created for relationship. Babies thrive when held; lives are longer when lived in community. Our need for relationship is why solitary confinement is one of the cruelest punishments endured in captivity. Compassion is ours in the beauty of relationships with God, ourselves, and people who are there to be with us, not to fix or judge us. That's what is so spectacular about Alcoholics Anonymous and similar support groups. They understand suffering and are uniquely able to give compassion without judging if relapse occurs. After giving compassion, they instill a sense of responsibility to uncover the thoughts, feelings, and change for a more sacred survival.

## THE FIX-IT SYNDROME

We often are stymied when we encounter people with harmful patterns of behavior. Our focus changes from compassion to fixing them. We like to fix things. We like closure and results. Our mind screams "Fix this! Do it my way!"

Tina was in touch with a friend every few days through email and phone calls. They shared many difficult things they were going through with their families, critical healthcare, and finances. It bothered Tina that each call began with her friend asking, "Anything new with you?" Tina told me, "It's as if she doesn't even hear me. Doesn't she remember any of the problems I shared with her? Tina finally confronted her friend, "Why do you ask me that when I tell you on each call how stressed out I am? Don't you care? I feel like you are ignoring me and my pain when you ask if anything is new." Her friend replied, "It's just that I think you are way too busy. I keep hoping that when I ask you if anything is new you'll say 'no.' You need to slow down and stop taking so much on. It's your own fault that you are stressed out."

This felt hard-hearted to Tina. When she needed compassion for her distress, she instead felt forced to defend her life, triggering additional suffering. She had to take care of her parents. She had to work long hours to make ends meet. She wanted to spend early mornings at worship. When her friend tried to fix her life by telling her to slow down, Tina felt forced to stand up for herself. This dialogue only resulted in a polite battle, guarding two very different survivals.

Compassion would have helped and healed. It might have sounded like, "Wow, it seems like you are going through a lot. It sounds rough. I'm sorry you are struggling. I'm sorry for your pain." In that sacred space and place of kindness, concern, and empathy, Tina could lower her defenses and feel the relief of someone helping her carry her pain. In that relief, she could consider new options rather than defending the ones that weren't working so well. If her friend co-suffered with her, together they might create a compassionate Sacred Survival.

Compassion shares the pain. It doesn't make the changes, but it can help make the change happen by taking some of the burden off those suffering. Then they can reinvest that energy into healing. Compassion doesn't condone the behavior. It says, "I'm going to co-pilot for a bit so you can focus on flying this plane and land it differently." Mostly, compassion offers love as sacred space and a sacred place to find renewal.

## COMPASSION FOLLOWS

Compassion doesn't lead. It follows. It never forces or manipulates. Compassion says to the one hurting (which could be yourself), "Let me hold some of your pain. It's too much for you to carry alone. I am here holding sacred space for you. I hurt when you hurt." Then the voice of compassion says, "I am here for you, but I cannot fix your situation. What do you want to do? You are in charge now. It's your move." Compassion doesn't actually lead people out of pain because it's up to the one hurting to make the move. However, compassion makes the move easier.

This is a little like making pizza dough or bread. You can push the dough all the way out to the edge of the pan. But the dough wants to shrink back. All the stretching and pushing won't make it go where you want it to go. As the recipe says, sometimes you just have to let the dough rest. It will rise in time.

## GIVE A LITTLE LOVE TO YOURSELF

We forget or are afraid to be compassionate with the person closest to us—ourselves. Maybe you're afraid you'll perpetuate your misery and get stuck in a black hole forever. So you pretend you aren't suffering until the voice of fear makes itself known at two in the morning. Trying to hide your fear is like pushing a beach ball down in the water. It keeps popping up. In order for you to receive compassion you have to let go of your fear and face some scary feelings. When you do, you will be much more open and willing to receive compassion.

> Fear screams, "Run away" from pain. Compassion whispers, "Come closer."

Without compassion, our pain misfires and shows up somewhere in the physical body. Mine shows up in neck pain and shallow breathing. Where does your pain show up? I mean literally. Where do you feel your suffering? Some of you feel it in your shoulders and clench your stomach muscles. Maybe you get migraines, TMJ, lower back pain, fever blisters, or bite your nails. The body never lies.

Sometimes the pain goes unnoticed until the body screams to be noticed. It's like a two-year-old asking for the prize in the sugary cereal box at the grocery store. You can ignore the request for only so long before a tantrum erupts in the middle of the store. If you are aware of where your body holds the emotional pain, you can look for it before you have a pain crisis. Check in with your body. It doesn't lie. It's your clue, your hint, and the evidence that you need some compassion. We are so used to your aches and pains that we ignore them. But like that two-year-old, the voice will get louder and louder until you stop and listen and make a choice about how to act. Compassion for yourself starts with more than knowing where it hurts; it is feeling where it hurts.

Kurt confided how hard it was to take care of his wife. People would tell him it could be worse. They told him to trust

God—and, my favorite—reminded him that God uses all things for good. I know, I know—true but trite clichés. The truth was, Kurt needed compassion because he was worn-out and worn-down from taking care of his paralyzed wife, whom he loved. He ignored his constant emotional strain until it showed up as intense back pain. He was unaware of the connection between his physical and emotional body. He didn't think he needed compassion—he thought he needed pain killers. Slowly we began to uncover his fears, anger, and loneliness. When he allowed himself to feel and accept those difficult feelings, he cried out and began a new way to survive. Whereas back pain could be medicated with pills, emotional pain required something else. When he recognized that he needed compassion and empathy, he let down his defenses that had prevented him from receiving it. He had confused asking for help as a sign of weakness or a show of faithlessness. But when he practiced sacred acceptance of his true thoughts and feelings, he was in position to practice sacred compassion: the giving and receiving of love that helped carry his pain, so he could carry on.

Fear screams, "Run away" from pain. Compassion whispers, "Come closer." When you listen to compassion, an amazing thing happens. You become stronger. Why? Because when someone gets close enough to carry your pain, you start freeing up emotional and physical energy to survive differently. The "someone" carrying your pain might even be you, when you allow yourself to experience self-care and true love. It might be the fifteen-year-old girl that still hurts in your fifty-five-year-old body. You can give her the compassion now that you couldn't when you were younger.

Practicing compassion on yourself is about having a conversation with your pain. Start with the pain you have identified in your body. If this is difficult to tap into, imagine how you feel hunger in your body. At times, you ignore it because you don't want to give in to it or you don't have time to take care of it. Or you have stuffed the appropriate feeling of hunger away. You have to wait for it and experience it to know how to feed yourself best. Pain is like that. You have to experience it and let yourself feel it so you know what it needs. Give your pain a voice. What is it trying to say? Let it speak. Then, speak back to it. Change your words from "Don't think about it" or "It's not that bad" or "No one cares" to "Yes, its lousy, it's unfair, it's painful. I believe you. It's real. I will carry some of it for you so you can survive differently."

## THE SHELTER OF COMPASSION

Tap into God's compassion and offer it to others as we do to ourselves. Treating strangers, friends, family, and foes as oneself is a holy state of seeing our lives in each other's. The suffering of others is our own suffering. It is about unselfishness, and loving others as ourselves. This doesn't happen well if we do not know how to love ourselves. Our hearts wait for compassion, and when it arrives, it shelters and cares for our suffering. In order to express compassion for others we have to be comfortable experiencing our own suffering. Without this comfort we will run from the pain of others, unable to feel anything but fear. Sacred compassion says, "No one is more worthy than you of compassion because you are created equally deserving of a beautiful life."

This is such a big goal. It is God-big. Compassion isn't just one of the sacred practices; it is the underpinning of all the other practices. Compassion is another word for love. Christian teachings are not the only spiritual guides that press us toward compassion. We may debate what we call God and how we seek God, but Jews, Muslims, Hindus, and Buddhists are also rooted in compassion and the prayer for merciful compassion.

## COMPASSION IS ANOTHER WORD FOR LOVE

Lack of compassion destroys individual lives and crumbles entire worlds. The opposite of compassion is more than indifference; it is abandonment. The opposite of compassion is the belief that "they" are not like "me," a lie that has justified genocides and holocausts. It is abandoning the disfigured and misfortunate homeless that we look past and walk by because fear screams, "Run away." Only compassion has healed the world's greatest atrocities. As much as we are individuals and unique, so we also feel that our suffering is unique, which erodes the spirit of compassion. This lonely feeling and this feeling that what we suffer is ours alone, is the very thing that keeps us from knowing how to extend compassion. We do not know how to relate our suffering to others and their suffering to ours. Compassion is engaged when we identify with others and share our feelings of loss for a common altruistic outcome.

> Compassion always protects, always trusts, always hopes, and always perseveres. Compassion never fails.

Relationships stir us to compassion. We are designed for compassion because we are designed to survive. It is the way we communicate. It is the love language of God spoken through His spirit through our spirit. 1 Corinthians 13 is frequently called the love chapter. It is commonly used during wedding ceremonies to describe the love God intended between two people. I wish we used these verses for every celebration of life.

I believe they are as much about love as they are about

compassion. If love is patient, is not compassion? If love is kind, is not compassion? It does not envy; it does not boast. Compassion does not dishonor and is not self-seeking. Compassion is not easily angered. It keeps no record of wrongs. Compassion does not delight in evil but rejoices in truth. Compassion always protects, always trusts, always hopes, and always perseveres. Compassion never fails.

## THOUGHTS TO CONTEMPLATE ABOUT COMPASSION

1. What are some other words for compassion? What do these have in common and how do they differ?

2. What is the difference between being compassionate and fixing a problem?

3. What is the purpose of compassion? Why is it the beginning of change and not the change itself? How does it help?

4. Why are you afraid to be compassionate?

5. How do you see your life in others and others' lives in yours?

NOTES:

CHAPTER EIGHT

# Relationships

At the beginning of each new chapter, I'm tempted to write, "Hey, this practice is the most important. It's the foundation for all the others. It's the chicken before the egg; the horse before the cart." For all my struggle to make the sacred practices linear and like steps up a ladder, they aren't and never will be. Each is the beginning, middle, end, and foundation of the others. The practices of Sacred Survival are more like an elevator ride, at some point starting and stopping at every floor, and going back again and again as necessary. Likewise, there is no direct route through Sacred Survival.

With all that said, the practice of relationship is a keystone to the others. This is where and how we live out our survival. However meager the neglect of other practices makes our existence, we could survive without them. But experience and history have proven we perish without relationships.

The basis for a Sacred Survival through relationship is

this: We are not only created to be in relationships; we are designed for supernatural relationships. The word *supernatural* is not found in the Bible. It didn't originate until the 16th century, and yet we use it often today to describe the characteristics and attributes of our biblical God. It is a superlative that denotes something above or beyond the natural. Many dictionaries describe it as unexplainable and abnormal. The word *abnormal* has a negative connotation today. We don't like abnormal things, things we can't explain or control, especially in relationships.

The upside of abnormal is that it also acknowledges something as special and outside our logical understanding. Thank God that our relationship with Him is supernatural, abnormal, beyond the limitations of our understanding, and existing outside of our restrictions. This sacred relationship is quite literally a lifesaver. These are the elements of supernatural that transform our normal relationships into sacred ones.

It doesn't matter if you're an introvert or an extrovert, a social butterfly or a wallflower. Sacred Survival depends on being in supernatural relationships that understand and accept that life goes deeper than ourselves. Sacred Survival depends on connecting to others at a "cellular" level. Like our own cells, these relationships provide structure and energy to thrive as a cohesive unit for a greater good. We feel the results of their regenerating power more than we see them, and their energy source propels us into a higher orbit of living. They seem beyond our explanation, and thankfully, they exist outside the limits we place on them.

Relationships function and dysfunction. They create both pain and pleasure. They make our survival miserable or miraculous and our lives heaven or hell. A lot of the times they make us feel like we're losing our mind. Is it easier to live a solitary life? Perhaps. Is it more sacred? Never. Remember, relationships are everything because they are the reason we are created. We can't avoid relationships because we are all in them with someone, somewhere. (Whether we acknowledge it or not, we are all in a relationship with our Creator and ourselves.)

> Relationships don't make us worthy but should remind us that we are.

A Sacred Survival depends on relational growth and healing if we are to live a better, deeper, and more significant life. Good relationships depend on good emotional health, and good emotional health depends on good relationships. Do you see the perpetual and problematic loop between relationships and our mental health? This is only the beginning of the snags we encounter in developing our sacred relationships.

## WHERE AND HOW RELATIONSHIPS GO WRONG

### 1. We don't know how to express our feelings or are impersonal when we do

Our technology has become one of the best ways to communicate and one of the best ways to stop communicating. An engaged couple came to see me for counseling. I fondly remember them as Mr. and Miss-understanding. They sat in my office with iPhones in their laps, their fingers and thumbs in position to text, swipe, pinch, and spread. Mr. and Miss-Understanding came in with their emails printed out for me to examine and give pronouncement of who was right and who was wrong. (Both of them were a little right and a little wrong, but refereeing debates is not my role as a counselor.) I was more curious about why they used emails and texts throughout the day to discuss some very important issues. I can't single them out. I have seen most of my clients communicate the same way. It may be efficient, but it's relationally dysfunctional and inappropriate because it takes most of the person out of the personal relationship. That's what my clients were doing: remaining distant because getting personal was too painful.

How many of us have heard or used that expression, "It's nothing personal." Or maybe you tried to calm someone down by saying, "It's just business." What's that about? Life is always personal. It never can be just about business. With all the great technology to Skype, text, and email, we keep personal human contact at a distance, We drive through everything from McDonald's to our relationships instead of going out of our way to make our human contact more personal.

## 2. We recycle our arguments

People come into my office for help settling their arguments—the kinds that keep happening over and over. They ask, "Why do we have the same argument? Why do I keep doing the same foolish thing in my relationships?"

Arguments are seldom about what we think they are. They're more likely about the relationship below the surface that needs attention. We lock into relationships at a superficial level because going deeper makes us uncomfortable. It's risky and stirs up past failures. Anytime we get near a conversation that makes us feel unsafe, we bounce back to a familiar argument to hide the heart of the problem. Sometimes, arguing about leaving the toothpaste cap off is a cover for feelings of neglect. It's a lot simpler to complain about being habitually late or not helping with the housework than to discuss the true conflict: "Why don't you respect me, or pay attention to me, or value me?"

When we have the same argument over and over, it may be because we're neglecting the real issue. To protect a tender wound, we try again by asking, "Why are you home so late from work all the time?" which is code for "I feel ignored and disrespected when you come home after 7 pm. Can we talk about how we can be more respectful toward each other?" When we brave the deeper waters of our feelings, our conversations will satisfy our needs and then our wants.

### 3. We isolate

We need relationships with other people. We don't live well when our only relationship is with ourselves. That's the same reason that a surgeon doesn't operate on himself: it's always painful and almost impossible. We need people like personal trainers at the gym and coaches at school because they help us become a better version of ourselves with others. The voices in our heads aren't always our best friends or the most accurate. And they are usually much less compassionate. So unless we have our own personal burning bush talking to us in the backyard like Moses did, we need people.

In the movie *Cast Away*, Tom Hanks's survival is so threatened by isolation that he develops an improbable friendship with a soccer ball that washes up on the island from his plane wreckage. "Wilson," the soccer ball, personifies a consciousness of himself, allowing him an alter ego to bounce off his thoughts and reflect his feelings. He needs Wilson to survive. He has found food and safety, but without relationship, he recognizes he is not really living. In the end, Hanks's character decides he would rather risk his life in a flimsy, make-shift raft in the middle of a threatening ocean than to be alone and isolated forever.

Without healthy relationships and the attention they provide, we care for ourselves in harmful ways. We defend our loneliness with every kind of behavior and justify all kinds of conduct, in all kinds of relationships. Loneliness justifies outrageous behaviors to get attention. When we are alone for too long or for the wrong reasons, extreme lifestyles play out in hope of making friends and having life-saving companionship. We don't just need people; we need the best people to help us be better people. Even if you think you are a solitary person, there are people all around you and in your life in subtle and meaningful ways. People come into your life for advice. People counsel you on TV shows and from the internet. People guide you even if they are channeling God's voice. People write the self-help books you read. People, people who need people, aren't just the luckiest people in the world; they are the most blessed people in the world. Even God was in a beautifully intricate, multidimensional relationship with Jesus and the Holy Spirit.

### 4. We are fooled by appearances

I was in church many years ago, sitting in my little wheelchair towards the back of the gym where we met. On that Sunday a visiting missionary spoke to us about his work overseas. Missionaries and people of faith are drawn to wheelchairs like there is some kind of magnetic force between them. They can't help making a connection. The missionary asked me if he could pray for my healing. He had no idea that I could stand and walk. He only saw the wheelchair, focused on my well-being, made some assumptions, and prayed that someday, by God's power, I would stand and walk again. I respected his heart and compassion, but it took all my composure to not stand, raise my arms, and pronounce my healing.

People are rarely who they appear to be. That is, who we are on the outside is rarely who we are in our hearts and souls. We are not always as we seem on the surface. If we don't take the time to scratch below it, we'll never uncover the "real" person. Recently, I met for lunch with an older man from my church. While we eyed pastries and drank tea and Pepsi, he said, "You know, it must be easy for those beautiful, young, healthy, talented people to sing their thanks and praises to God on stage every Sunday morning. It's a lot harder for us when the world has fallen apart." I agreed. It does look easy for them. From a distance, some people do seem untouched by the world's pain. But I know, and God knows, the unspeakable sadness and tragedy they've already endured. They are surviving loss, death, abandonment, and hurt behind those big smiles. People are rarely who or what they appear to be. Next to you now, someone is hurting without showing it. And someone is ready to help you when you least expect it.

## HOW DO WE MAKE OUR RELATIONSHIPS SACRED?

### 1. Lean in and pay attention

I believe there is a common denominator in our make-up that I call the attention factor. It's a theory I have written about for the last decade. We are all born needing attention—lots of attention. From the minute we are born, we literally cry out for it to remind people we need them to survive. As we grow older and more self-conscious, we stop asking people for attention and paying ourselves the kind of attention we need. We think it makes us weak or proud. It's just the opposite. Attention validates our worth. We don't have to DO anything to be worthy; we already are because we belong to God. Relationships don't make us worthy but should remind us that we are.

God apparently is big on socializing. Most of His creations are social creatures—less than a dozen animals on this earth live alone. I am reminded by God's first recorded words to man after creation that it is not good for man to be alone. If we don't connect to other people, we suffer. We live a life that isn't fully alive. The attention we need is found in many forms as simple eye contact, being friended on Facebook, getting the promotion on the job, or being picked for the team when you could have been left standing on the side of the gym. Without attention or with the wrong type of attention, our survival becomes so strained that we make friends with whomever or whatever we can.

> Keep your eyes open and your heart open wider.

Attention is good. It is what we need to understand our neuroses. It is what we get when we get into relationships. Jesus pays us all kinds of attention and ultimately lays down his life for us! That's a relationship. In relationships we either push each other away or draw each other closer with everything we do or say. Anything we can do to avoid turning away or against each other matters. Then, even when we are in conflict, we are close enough to resolve or dissolve our problems. In the "togetherness," anything is possible. Togetherness grows when we pay attention to each other. Attention is a wonderful thing. But it's how you get it and what you do with is that makes your relationships more sacred.

My husband and I have developed a creative and crucial practice of asking for attention when we need it. We don't make each other guess. Experience has taught us that when we make our friends and family guess what we want, they almost always guess wrong. So I say to him, "I need some attention today." And he asks, "How much? A little or a lot?" He opens his hands to show a little and then wider, like showing me a big fish he caught. "This much," I say, pointing to his outstretched hands. We don't guess, try to interpret, or compete with each other for what we need. We lean in and pay attention.

## 2. Relate face to face

Nothing heals better than personal contact and "being in the moment." Being in the moment is mindful, intentional, and personal. It's where relationships live. Getting personal can be uncomfortable. We avoid face-to-face confrontation and eye contact by using email and voice mail. It is so much easier to text "No," the ultimate last word in an argument, than say it in person. I often put my counseling clients on a two-week technology fast. I challenge them to go without texting, emailing, and voice mail for anything other than "shop-talk." Shop-talk sounds like, "Pick up some milk on your way home," and "I'll be home at six tonight." I challenge them to use face-to-face communication for "heart-talk." This sounds like, "I resent that you always forget I have lactose intolerance," and "Why are you always late? Don't you want to see me?"

Then I challenge them to go one step further. I suggest they avoid drive-through banking, ATMs, and drive-through fast food restaurants. This is a spiritual discipline as much as anything. The idea is to make our daily communication personal with person-to-person interaction, eye contact, and handshakes. The idea is to shower people with attention, to recapture and build intimacy. Without this ability, we create a superficial familiarity instead of the personal intimacy God wants.

## 3. Know and be known

When we are in relationship, we show up for each other. How much easier it is to show up for those we know or love. I am more likely to help people that I know. I am even more likely to help people that I love. And as far as those people that I cherish as beloved—well, I can't get there fast enough! The sacred practices of acceptance and compassion are more likely to be expressed toward those who are part of our community—in our family, neighbors, in our social organizations, or in our places of worship. That's why when we are asked to help those we don't know, we are shown their pictures and told their stories. Compassion International sends me a photo of the child I help support to keep her sweet face and needs in front of me. Her picture sits among my other family photos so she starts to feel like part of my own. When we talk about our church ministry or our Africa missions, we show the faces of the lives we are changing. This helps us connect with each other. That is human nature—and our God's nature—that desires to connect always in a life-changing, meaningful relationship. Our relationships with each other and with God are special. We are beloved. In that capacity and from that position we can love others and show up for them with sacred practices.

Relationships are strengthened by support and understanding. People don't come to my counseling office only for answers. (A good thing because I don't give answers; I usually just stir up more questions.) They want to begin to understand themselves. Even more, they want to be understood by others. There is something special and helpful about being understood. Unfortunately, true understanding is hard to come by, not because people don't want to understand your pain and problems, but because they can't unless they have gone through something very similar. They can, however, give you something else that is equally valuable. They can be there holding sacred space for you, giving you compassion, and carrying our pain in ways that are both functional and spiritual. They can pray with you, stay up with you, cry with you, and prepare meals for you along with anything else that will make your suffering easier. And you can surround them with care and compassion the same way. This is a beautiful, healing kind of attention you can give each other when you are present together in relationship.

### 4. Live in the moment

Can you live in the moment? This is really the only moment that we live in. T. S. Eliot wrote that life is not isolated intense moments with a before and after—it is a lifetime burning in every moment. My pastor, Stan Mitchell of GracePointe Church, helped me reconstruct my life of faith and hope when he described the beauty of every ending as a beginning, only possible because we took an exit that set us free. To make those exits, we have to live in the moments and feel the burn of the moment. A Sacred Survival depends on living in the moment, and the next, and the next. Sacred relationships seek living in the present instead of ruminating over the past or fearing for the future. When we pay attention to each other with purpose, using all our senses, we can't help but make them more personal. It is in those moments that we practice awareness, acceptance, and compassion because we get in touch with our needs and desires. Paying attention to each other is an extension of how we take care of ourselves. When we love ourselves and give our lives the kind of care and healthy attention they deserve, we are better able to do so for each other. Many of us don't like ourselves enough to do that. We avoid taking care of ourselves and so are not prepared to take care of others moment by moment in the "here and now." The way we keep company with ourselves is based, in part, on how wounded and hurt we are, making us feel ugly and unworthy from past crises that have become chronic problems. We have sacrificed forgiveness, trust, and hope and are left with defensiveness and vulnerability, unable to see anything but the past or worry about the future. Sacred relationships stay present in the moments of new beginnings, where awareness, acceptance, and compassion heal. Keep your eyes open and your heart open wider.

### 5. We hold sacred space for people

Holding a sacred space with sacred silence is to hold another's pain with a compassion that doesn't try to fix or judge. This is one of the reasons support groups are so effective. There is unique understanding in the presence of relapse and failure. There is compassion that renews another's strength while still holding the other accountable to let go and go on to be better. That's why AA works. That's why Al-Anon works and Sampson, cancer groups, and parenting groups work. A support group might be the person you run with at the gym or the mom you meet in the nursery. Support groups bring people together where they can say, "I know. I know how you feel. I know your pain and I will hold some of it for you."

Who created the first support group? Well, it may have been God. God was and is always there for us. He took his support another dimension deeper when He became infinitely more relatable. He became like us. He became a man who could say to us, "I know. I know your pain. I cry. I am disappointed. I am rejected. I hurt. I understand." If you're looking to connect with the one who can truly understand you, join His support group. Thank God it isn't anonymous.

### 6. It's not all about us

Relationships reflect how we relate to ourselves, which influences how we connect with each other, either as beauties or beasts. We may have a few deep relationships and many simple but meaningful friendships. The redwood forests give us a wonderful metaphor about the way every relationship counts. Redwood trees can grow hundreds of feet tall, but their root system is not very deep. Simple engineering theory tells us that such tall trees should not be able to remain standing with their root system. But further study of their roots reveals their secret: by growing close together and intermingling their root systems, they stand tall and strong, often for over a thousand years. We can go deep in relationship, or we can stretch out and hang on to each other. Either way, we need each other for maximum power and growth.

We are in a sacred relationship with God not because it changes who HE is but because it can change who WE are. Sometimes it changes us in ways we don't expect. In this kind of relationship we will have a greater understanding of who we are, how we are living, and who is the God we worship and follow.

## 7. Choose carefully

One of the easiest, and most difficult, question to answer is, "Are you ready to take responsibility for your relationships?" These are the precious lives that get buried underneath everything from our survival crisis to mediocrity. If there's anything I hope I have impressed on you, it is that working on your relationships isn't a last resort when everything else has failed. Sacred Survival seeks constant growth and improvement in relationships. It is grounded in the model of the supernatural relationship we have with God.

When and how do we take responsibility for our relationships? It happens moment by moment, depending on whom we surround ourselves with. Do we surround ourselves with the people who give good counsel and attention and are in the fight with us? I am careful whom I take with me on my journey. My husband is my first choice. I once asked him, "Why do you love me? I mean, why? I'm an awful lot to take care of."

"Yes, you are," he said with a smile. "But I love you because

I love you. It's not because of anything. I just love you." In this performance-based world, that was just about the nicest thing I had ever heard. Then he said, "Do you know why you love me?"

"Why?" I whispered.

"You love me because you're like a bird. You love to fly. And in our home, I keep the window open so you can fly."

Who is helping you fly? Who do you surround yourself with that keeps the window open? Who will help you take the next step of untangling the strings that hold you down? Sacred relationships accept you now, AND believe the best in you is yet to come.

I live by the proverb, "Who we are with is who we become." Whoever we walk with affects how we walk. Imagine you are running a three-legged race. You are 4 foot 9 inches and your partner is 6 foot 4 inches. Either he will pull you along, or you will hold him back to your stride. You accommodate each other. All relationships are that way. We are the average of the people we surround ourselves with. In other words, some people have a positive effect on us and other people have a negative effect. This doesn't mean that they aren't valuable, but their effect on us might not be. Even if they are great people, they may rub us the wrong way. It is important to assess if those we spend time with have a positive or a negative effect on us. We can't always remove the negative influences in our lives, but we can add positive relationships to our world that make us glad we are surviving.

## HOW DOES THIS WORK?

A few weeks ago my husband and I made the drive up to the summit of Mount Haleakula on the Hawaiian Island of Maui. One of the two dormant volcanoes that erupted thousands of years ago, it formed the island that is now our treasured paradise. The summit brochure used the word "sacred" five times to describe the physical grandeur, the spiritual presence, and the holy responsibility we have to connect the earth with the spirit. We left the hotel at 8 a.m. with the expectation to see something beautiful and spiritual.

The drive in our little red Mustang convertible began at sea level, at 8 a.m., and at 80 degrees. Over the next two hours, we would make the ascent up to 10,000 feet, where the temperature dropped to 49 degrees, the air was thin, and the view was from above the clouds looking down—way down. We drove. We climbed. I sat in the passenger side, closest to the edge of the winding road. When I say "close," I mean that I could look thousands of feet down only inches away from the edge.

My body surprised me with a tight, twisting feeling in my stomach. That I was nervous was an understatement. If we weren't careful, we would certainly go over the edge, where there were no guardrails, only signs warning us of falling rocks. I found myself leaning toward the middle of the car, willing it toward the road's center line Yeah, like that would help.

We passed bicyclists, careening downhill from their sunrise tour. They wore heavy-duty helmets with little cameras up front, thick gloves, and boots. They flew around the mountain's curve crossing over the centerline; I extended my leg, pushing down on an invisible brake pedal and willing the car to slow down. Yeah, like that would help.

Along the way, we passed small areas where cars could pull over for a photo op (or a merciful chance to turn around and descend to where mere mortals live.) I saw buses filled with Asian tourists with impressive photo equipment. Like a scene from Mary Poppins, they artfully unfolded their tripods from small satchels, and pulled out lights and teapots.

They captured their memories with the beautiful photography equipment: heavy zoom lens, light meters, and flashes. Standing next to them was a group of young American teenagers with their smart phones, iPhones, and iPads. They stood with their arms outstretched attempting to zoom in on the distant view in lieu of having a traditional zoom lens. Yeah, like that would help.

A few times on the way up—when I opened my eyes—I would spontaneously gasp at the view and say, "Wow!" My husband turned to look. I shouted, "Keep your eyes straight ahead! You can look later. Right now your only job is to stay in your lane." I didn't want him to look back, look around, or look too far ahead. I figured yelling at him would help him drive. Yeah, like that would help.

We arrived at the summit two hours later. The air was so thin that my lungs burned. We got out of the car, found our legs and my stomach, and took a moment to acknowledge that we arrived. "Whew, we made it." Now, this is a national park that thousands, maybe millions of people have safely visited. I'm fairly certain that not everyone had the strong reaction to the dizzying heights and twisted drive that I did. But the reason I am sharing my reaction to the journey is this: I survived the experience, and in this simple survival, discovered sacred relationship principles.

First, it was a reminder that when we are frightened and feel threatened, our thoughts and feelings get confused. Just like the trip up the summit, some relationships make us feel unsafe and confused. Sometimes that confusion or anxiety shows up in our body's physical reaction. It becomes difficult to express ourselves verbally so the feelings show up physically. It was hard for me to remain present on the drive up, but the body doesn't lie. In survival mode, the brain gives way to the body's flight-or-fight response. The parasympathetic and sympathetic nervous system kicks in, rerouting the blood from the cerebral functioning to the large muscles so that the body can run. Everything in my body told me to run away from this danger. My body had a visceral reaction, and I leaned in toward the center of the road to keep the car from getting too close to the edge. My muscles were flexed to catch myself from an imagined fall. I've learned that when my heart races or my stomach tightens in a relationship, to ask if there is something else going on than what meets the eye. I've learned that my physical reactions are trying to tell me, "Pay attention. Breathe deeply. Wait for the blood to return to the part of your brain where decisions are properly made." This drive reminded me that sometimes we stop thinking and feeling in scary relationships and have to do everything we can to return to the present where the relationships are real.

> We are in a sacred relationship with God not because it changes who HE is. We do it because it can change who WE are in ways we don't expect.

Secondly, this trip reminded me that I would not have easily survived if I had driven alone. I might not have even taken the trip to Hawaii if not encouraged to join my husband. We are better off when we don't go it alone. As my husband kept his eyes in front of him, I could be his rear view mirror and long distance view. I could be his zoom lens and his playback feature to share what was coming and what we just survived. If he didn't stay in the moment and stay present, our survival might have unraveled differently. When we are in relationships, we help each other see when the other's pain blurs their view. We are more likely to embark upon experiences that stretch us and expand our lives. Without relationships, we overlook or miss opportunities. With each other, we create context and memories that encourage us to wrap our "roots" around each other for incredible heights in living.

Third, this experience didn't just benefit me; it created an experience that I could use to relate to others. Many of our experiences aren't merely about our own happiness. The more we experience, the more we are able to relate to others with compassion because we can see our similarities instead of thinking we are not alike. When we find our lives in others and see their lives in ours, then we are headed toward a compassionate relationship.

Fourth, I remembered that things are not always what they appear to be. We have to consider different perspectives and consider that others use a different lens to experience the world. The view from behind the long telescopic lens was very different from the perspective of the young adults with their smart-phone cameras. Each leaned in to their own viewpoint, which was not the same as mine. Nor could I imagine what they were seeing from their point of view. Each view has value and says as much about the outlook as it does about the one who is looking. Relationships are like that—everyone's view is unique and  is defined as much by the view as the viewer.

Finally, I'm glad I chose my driving companion carefully. Sometimes who we survive with is a matter of life and death. In that car, and in life, we are better when everyone gets the attention (respect, love, value) that they want and need. We are created to connect. It is our life force. The car wasn't very comfortable that day, and it reminded me that when we aren't comfortable in our own "skin" we will be uncomfortable in relationships with others. How can you get comfortable in the relationship you have with yourself?

## RELATIONSHIPS BELIEVE IN YOU

Relationships grow more sacred in a life filled with shared hopes and visions. The media is filled with superheroes and superstars that shout encouragement like, "Carpe Diem" (*Dead Poets Society*) and, "Step up to the plate and write your story forward" (*Lord of the Rings*) and "I'm king of the world" (*Titanic*). Sacred relationships believe in your royalty. They believe that you are kings and queens created in this kingdom for great works and great love. Supernatural relationships say, "I believe in you, seize the day, and step up to your Sacred Survival." Supernatural relationships don't keep score, or say "I told you so," or hold you back. They say, "I will help you fly."

## THOUGHTS TO CONTEMPLATE ABOUT RELATIONSHIPS

1. List the five people that you spend the most time with (not the most important people, but those you are with the most). On average, do you feel better or worse when you are with each of them? What do you have to do to bring your average up?

2. Write about or discuss the theory, "Who you are with is who you become."

3. What makes you feel more isolated and what makes you feel more connected to people? How can you intentionally create connections in your life?

NOTES:

# CHAPTER NINE

# Exits

## THE PARADOX OF BEGINNINGS AND ENDINGS

At first glance, it seems that the practice of exits in a Sacred Survival is a paradox. Isn't God about creating, beginning—not ending? We love entering new stages of life. Our spiritual lives take on a special quality of renewal, recreation, and rebirth. Our day-to-day lives are filled with invitations, openings, and introductions. We establish and found new businesses and homesteads. And isn't survival about endurance, hanging on, and staying power? Exits mean goodbyes, quitting, and the end of something. That doesn't sound like survival, sacred or otherwise.

So why exits? Because life is also a series of letting go, acknowledging an ending so that we can begin again. Exits set us free. One of the most important practices in our continual renewal of life is to make sacred exits. What matters is that we find a way to say goodbye to what has served us well, or hurt us badly, so we can let go and go on to a Sacred Survival.

The practice of sacred exits is the discovery of making a good goodbye, the kind that will set us free.

## OUR GRAND EXITS

What do we exit in life? We leave relationships, jobs, homes, and school. We leave stages of life, our youth, and our physical abilities as muscles give way to aging and atrophy. Sometimes we leave people or places without even realizing we have because it's a natural journey towards something new as much as it is leaving something valuable behind. Other times, the goodbye is tragic and regrettable. Whichever, we are usually ill-prepared for making a smooth and healthy exit. Our leave-takings are extremes, from the hurried and abrupt (often unspoken) goodbye to the agonizingly slow one where our ineptness for healthy exits has held us far too long. Both ways, we are doing it badly. We leave badly because we stay badly. And by the time we leave, we are in crisis.

A sacred exit is not only about why and what you leave; it is about how you say goodbye. Making an exit should not be an automatic impulse or something we do whenever we feel uncomfortable. If you recognized yourself in the Acceptance chapter as one who withdraws and runs from pain and conflict, then sacred exits are particularly complicated for you.

We are taught very few lessons about saying goodbye. We may learn the hard way—out of necessity and through experience—how to leave and how to leave something or someone. But I know of no formal training course in exiting. There are courses in start-ups, business launches, how to begin a marriage, how to jumpstart a diet, and how to start and raise a family. Our culture applauds the spirit, gumption, and promise of new beginnings. We admire entries, new plans, and embarking on new adventures. We give kudos to entrepreneurs who pave the new way.

By contrast, our exits are often overlooked, invisible, and denied. We seldom praise people for leaving something or someone. When we move out or on, we receive little support and understanding. Perhaps others don't want to acknowledge something that they are afraid of doing themselves. So we steal away, hoping no one will notice. We mirror it in our posture and bearing. In the beginning, we stand straight and move strong, proud and determined; at the exit, we shuffle away, stooped over, weakened, with eyes averted. Of course, this is as much because some leave-takings are so very hurtful and unfortunate.

Hear me. This is not a proposal for unwarranted divorce or suicide. This is a thoughtful look at making the kind of exits that will set us free. It is not only about what we leave, but what we

> We leave badly because we stay badly. And by the time we leave, we are in crisis.

are going toward: a Sacred Survival filled with the strengths, acceptance, compassion, and relationships that some situations, people, and places prevent us from having. We can leave harmful groups, lifestyles, and relationships. We have the choice to say goodbye to the things in life we cannot hold on to, like our youth and our grown children. Life is a series of letting go.

In our contemporary culture, where we make as many or more exits than entrances, I am concerned that we are relatively unpracticed and uncomfortable with the endings of our lives. More than half of marriages end in divorce with tortured endings. The average length of a job is five years. Not only will we have multiple jobs, we will have multiple careers. Wars end and soldiers leave traumatic lives where they feared and faced unspoken goodbyes every day. Decade to decade, we leave one stage of life for the next. And as much as we are created with a strong survival instinct, we begin dying the day we are born. We are often publically exposed when we exit something or someone, and privately endure the pain of it—not because leaving was wrong, but because we are shamed into thinking we are quitters. Waiting too long, for too little to go on to, we are often forced into humiliated exits. The expression, "If you can't handle the heat, get out of the kitchen" sends the insensitive message that we couldn't handle it. It is because of these hidden and not so hidden messages that I practice the power of good "goodbyeing."

## WHY GOODBYES ARE UNNATURAL

The origin of the word *goodbye* is from the mid-1500s. It was a contraction of the expression, "God be with ye." It is essential that we learn how to make worthy beginnings after graceful goodbyes. What sets sacred exits apart from ordinary departures is that they take God with them. Our world so avoids saying goodbye that kids postpone their exits—psychologists describe it as a failure to launch. Adults prefer to "keep the door open" in case they change their mind. Social media makes it difficult to say final goodbyes, even if we want to. Just when an old relationship dissolves in our memory, a "friend" request materializes on our social media site. We even avoid saying goodbye, and text it instead. An electronic goodbye is the ultimate final word. And finally the ultimate exit of physical death may lack the respectful attention, rituals, and honor it deserves.

Leaving the familiar, especially when we are leaving the roles that have shaped our identity and self-image, can be excruciating. Sometimes we must exit the work that gave us opportunity, authority, and privilege. We live within the tension of staying put and moving on. But with the huge build up of beginnings where dreams are dreamed and hope springs eternal, our exits cannot help but appear sad and even shameful in comparison.

Exits are rare in this technological world. The boundaries between public and private, intimate and distant, have been redrawn. We begin messaging those we left about the schedule we forgot, or directions, or something we should have said in person as soon as we pull out of the driveway. When the kids start college, they text their parents with pictures and icons throughout the day to describe their new beginning that won't let go of their past. When kids go to camp, videos and vimeos are sent to their parents depicting each accomplishment, art project, and sing-along. With every YouTube post there is the opportunity to connect with a memory and stay in that moment, again and again. I'm not saying this is all bad. However, it is clear that our exits have become blurred. Exit boundaries have become harder to define and harder to practice. Even our deaths have indistinct borders now. Our organs can be technically alive and our hearts continue to beat, even though we have evidence of brain death.

As a researcher in this field, I am particularly interested in how our practices for exits are continually rewritten, retold, and remembered. Especially in dying, we strive for ways to do it differently, albeit better. Again, I am struck by the sense of entitlement the American culture has to live and die better than our parents and grandparents. Perhaps that extends to claiming better deaths and dying experiences. The way we think and talk about life and death is the foundation for decision-making and for the pathways we embark on, and stay on, to survive until we decide that we no longer want to or are able to. We are created and wired to survive.

Are there rituals to practice that could light a path toward the healthy exit? Can you begin again if you haven't left? Too often we try to have it both ways by straddling two worlds, but living in neither fully. What freedom do you seek? What do you need to exit for that freedom? Exits can be liberating, but only if they are well-navigated.

## A GOOD OR BAD GOODBYE

Some exits are too abrupt—we want to fix something, move on, get over it, and deny our feelings about the loss. This is troubling in a Sacred Survival that requires honesty and acceptance of feelings. Exits should be done thoughtfully and deliberately. Thoughtful doesn't mean getting stuck in the revolving door. Thoughtfulness manifests as a sense of responsibility and dignity. Survival is about leaving what threatens us, not because we don't have the coping mechanisms for conflict and tension but because our sacred life is at risk. Exiting a relationship has as much to do with you as it does the one you are leaving. Imagine giving purpose to your exit as you and the ones you are leaving take time to share your thoughts and feelings.

Alan left his company after twenty years of employment. Although the leaving was his choice, he struggled with feelings of loss—loss of his identity, his power, and his dream of the security he thought he would have by that time. These losses, ambiguous and unpredictable, were evident in his thoughts and his posture. He sent out a short email thanking a few people he directly worked with. He planned on leaving at noon to avoid emotional and awkward goodbyes at the end of the day. He projected his discomfort onto his coworkers. His coworkers wanted to say, "Good luck and we'll miss you." But Alan's anxiety convinced him that no one would miss him and it would be easier to avoid a personal goodbye. They wanted to wish him well and make plans for a reunion. Alan never knew. He didn't have the other Sacred Survival skills of strength, acceptance, compassion, and relationship that could help him make a good goodbye.

It is important to let those we are leaving express their anger or sadness, or allow them space to express their love and affection. Making a good goodbye creates dignity and respect for yourself and for those you leave. But if we cannot feel our own loss and cannot be comfortable in our feelings of sadness or worse, we will not be able or willing to allow others to express their feelings to us.

Sometimes others leave us with mean-spirited and cruel farewells. We are poorly prepared to carefully listen and absorb their words. Alan's replacement, Tim, spoke of Alan's prior work and efforts with disrespect. He boasted about the plans he was making to "improve" Alan's department. His remarks were not indicative of who Alan was but who Tim was: insecure and afraid. His words pointed to his own lack of confidence even as he directed them at Alan. They were both saying goodbye in a different way. Tim was leaving his safety net. Alan was leaving his role and everything his identity afforded him. The listening part of a goodbye is as important as the speaking part of the goodbye. In a healthy goodbye, they could listen to each other without interrupting, without defending their positions, without trying to convince and change the other. Listening is a matter of respect, not the pause before launching a counterattack. Listening receives the other's feelings and holds them compassionately so the other person is free to consider other thoughts and actions. Listening quiets the mind so there is space to consider what the words stir up, what reactions occur, and what alternative healthy reactions are possible.

## A GOOD GOODBYE IS...

You might be removing yourself from the role of a caretaker, the CEO, the wife, the student, the overprotective mom, or the constant hostess. You might be leaving your servanthood at church that has grown too exhausting. You might be growing older and leaving behind the vitality and energy you've been accustomed to. Recalibrating your relationships with others and yourself helps you discover new options. If you leave badly, you will have regrets, not about what or why you left, but how you left. Only when you leave well will you have the energy and imagination to compose your next beginning. Setting yourself free in an exit uses a new approach to finding who you are and what you value the most. This is the essence and purpose of your existence.

> If you withdraw and run from pain and conflict, then sacred exits are particularly complicated for you.

## NO EXPECTATIONS

A client asked me what a good goodbye looks like. I answered that it has no expectations. It is a release without expecting something back. We often say goodbye with the agenda or hope, "Now they will miss me. Maybe this will make them sorry. I bet they will chase me down with the apology I deserve." This kind of exit does not set us free. This kind keeps us dependent on their response. We stay in the relationship, even though we have physically left, trying to read their minds and figure out their next moves so we can protect ourselves. This is the classic definition of codependency. In trying to control the goodbye, we end up being controlled by the situation we are leaving.

## FOR EVERYONE'S BEST

The good goodbye focuses and appreciates what is good for everyone. It asks, "How has this situation or relationship served me?" and, "How can I make meaning out of this relationship, in one way or another?" You are in charge of that exit, not them. When you say a good goodbye, you are no longer controlled by what you left. There are no "if only" and "what if" remnants controlling your future.

## OFFERS FORGIVENESS

A good goodbye has sacred elements of forgiveness for all. Forgiveness doesn't always include trust or keeping the door open for a continual kind of slavery. It does provide the possibility and benefit of preserving memories that are nourishing and renewing for the future. We may exit because we are leaving something harmful or because we are moving toward another stage of life. There is a difference, however, between codependency and cherishing the good memories and making use of what helped us grow and mature. Too many people think that their exits need to be all or nothing. It is a careful practice to leave what is necessary while keeping what is beautiful. That's what a sacred exit looks like. It savors how someone or something was good in our lives, either by shaping our beliefs, protecting us at that time, or resulting in tangible gain. This is not the same thing as keeping one foot in an old relationship and another in a new relationship. This knows what to let go of and what to hold on to. This is not the same thing as the ends justifying the means. This is a practice at the road's end that reaches back and grabs hold of the best parts. If any cliché applies, it is "don't throw the baby out with the bath water." Underneath all the dirty water may be something important and worth saving.

## TRANSFORMS THE EXPERIENCE

When we exit, we never are the same because of the experience. But when we leave, or exit, we wear the experience in our hearts and souls differently. We transform what might have been difficult and wear it as helpful. We can transform a sorrowful departure of youth or good health into an important appreciation for a new beginning. We make meaning out of what we left behind by keeping the best part in front of us. It is not an either-or situation. We can be happy and sad at the same time.

Anna was in a long on-and-off relationship with Joe, a married man. The relationship went through the typical stages from romance to reality. At every opportunity for her to exit the relationship, she remained and was abused, and controlled by him. Joe had all the power because of Anna's past experience of abandonment. Why couldn't Anna leave this relationship? She was stuck in her past reactions of being left countless times as a child and well into her adult life. Parents, men, bosses, and friends had left her, creating a significant deficit in self-worth. Without her realizing it, all her relationships revolved around her efforts to keep others from leaving her. Her every effort and word was carefully scripted and acted to control them. The child in her repeated in her mind, "Please don't go," or, "What can I do to make you stay?"

Ironically, when her first husband did stay, she didn't want him. The fact that he remained in her life didn't satisfy her deep longing to feel that she had some control over those who threatened to leave her. She needed to know that if people threatened to leave, she could change their mind. She thought that was the only way to protect herself. It was only in that dynamic that she felt the safety and security of knowing she held the power over her destiny. Therefore, every time Joe left her, either physically or emotionally, she doubled her efforts to get him back. There was no letting him go. Only the constant struggle to get him back gave her hope that she had some power over being hurt. Occasionally, she would see him for his cruelty. But when she took the steps to leave, it was always with the hope that he would miss her or be sorry and beg her to stay. So there was no true goodbye. She remained dependent on convincing him that she was worth keeping. This tether was strangling her.

Those who had previously abandoned her, physically or emotionally, still had a hold on her. Her good goodbye depended on her getting them out of her life, even if they only lived in her head. Her new freedom depended on her being able to survive her past feelings, leave them, and choose a new reaction that would help her embrace a new identity. So she said goodbye to her fifteen-year-old self who had been abandoned by her father. That girl had remained in her head trying to protect her. Now she could say goodbye to her, stronger and able to take care of her forty-year-old self. Her exit from her ffiteen-year-old broken self became the onramp to her new beginning.

Goodbyes trouble us. Even when we think we have said a final goodbye to someone or something, a part of us remains with them, and they with us. It's a little haunting. Maybe we had no power over someone leaving us. They may have left us without warning. They may have died or killed themselves. Maybe we agonize over how we could have made them stay, or we left the door open just in case. But a good goodbye closes the door without fear that a monster is on the other side.

## THE REMAINS OF THE GOODBYE

We can't make what we are leaving completely disappear. Even if we let it go, it will forever be woven into our life. But we can transform its presence in our life and wear it differently. When people ask me to help them make their memories disappear, to make their "enemy vanish," I help them discover a way to exit that transforms the past. I give them an ice cube that represents what they are trying to forget, and tell them to wrap their fingers around it and describe what they feel. Of course, they always say it's cold. Some say it's burning, and uncomfortable, or that it stings, sticks to the skin, and is sharp. I tell them that this is the person, place, or thing that they are leaving. This is what they are saying goodbye to. Then I ask them to notice what is happening to the ice cube. They acknowledge it is melting. They say, "It isn't as cold anymore. They edges are softer. It's getting smaller and easier to hold." I explain that this is what happens when we leave something. We don't make it disappear. We transform it. It will always be around in some shape, but we can transform it into something more tolerable, even beautiful and useful in our life. There will be circumstances that freeze the water into an ice cube again. In that situation, we use the practice of warming and transforming once more. And I always ask, "Did you get any on you? I mean, did you get a little wet?" Of course they did. That's what happens with leaving. We always get a little of what we left on us or in us. Whatever we are exiting gets absorbed into our skin. It will forever be a part of us. And like water, it can nurture us in some small way if only as something we can exhale in the practice of breathing and feeling alive. Tired of hanging on to the past? Letting go doesn't mean we have to forget everything. We can hang on to the parts that helped us without letting them control us.

## SAYING YOUR GOODBYES

Now, who or what are you thinking about leaving? Imagine this person sitting across from you in an empty chair. If this is too threatening or uncomfortable, envision writing a letter to them with all the truth you can summon. You don't ever have to actually speak to them or give the letter. Just putting together the words that express your true thoughts and feelings begins a sacred exit. It is sacred because it is uncovering what you haven't gotten to think, feel, and accept. Maybe the goodbye was one-sided in the past. You never were given a chance to respond. Perhaps your first thoughts and feelings were shock and the real ones have only recently surfaced, making them available and ready to accept and share. Sometimes the voices in your head were confused, angry, and defensive, preventing you from knowing how to say goodbye. Or maybe what you said before was an effort to extract a certain response from them—not what you wanted to say, but what you thought would satisfy your needs.

Now is the time to find your true voice that will answer the question, "What do you need to set yourself free?" This kind of freedom isn't selfish and careless. It doesn't abandon others or who you are meant to be. It is the freedom of knowing you are released from who you pretended to be and what you defended yourself from. When you let go of the false hope that your exit will control others, you are letting go of the control that they have over you. This is a sacred exit because it isn't made only as a response to pain, but in pursuit of what is good and right. You exit because in spite of what others might say and do, it is the right thing to do. These exits leave no trailing questions of, "What if I had left this way instead?" They rest on their rightness.

Try to imagine what your goodbye sounds like. Do you imagine hearing an angry or painful response? If you let their reaction silence what must be said for a sacred exit, you may be settling for a goodbye that fears conflict. Instead, imagine their feelings and write a goodbye that is kind and honest. It doesn't have to be one way or the other. The purpose of imagining their response is to stay present in your pain, even if you're uncomfortable, and summon your compassion that will heal and transform the goodbye. Do you hear anger, abandonment, sorrow or love and understanding? Just listen. You do not have to convince them that you are right or they were wrong. Leave the expectations you have at the door you walk out of.

## CLOSE YOUR EYES, OPEN YOUR HEART.

When God enters and exits, He has both His eyes and His heart open. Our physical response to fear and pain is to close our eyes. We close them when we cry, fall, and can't bear to see something or someway slip away. But so many times we imagine a monstrous disaster in the wake of leaving when it is really a manageable departure. The good goodbye is at home in the heart. So even if you close your eyes, a good goodbye keeps your heart open wide.

Our history of patterns and responses, coupled with dreams and hopes, keeps us hooked on what we know rather than exploring the mystery of what could be. We usually choose history over mystery until the pain of staying is so deeply ingrained that we cannot imagine a future without it. Then we finally are able to leave. Even then, we choose to repeat a painful life we know over an uncertain new way of living. Mystery is hard. Every game, science experiment, and movie teaches us that we must solve the mystery. The only way we can solve the mystery of what is on the other side of the exit is to exit. We have an imagination not to fear but to hope. It lets us hope, hope, and hope more. It lets us rewrite our story with a happier ending.

## THE ABSURDITY OF DEATH: THE ULTIMATE GOODBYE

We do not appreciate the pain of our exit if we can help it. I mean into our innermost self. Our worlds have such a grasp on us with its busy, demanding days that we are not able to fully experience the most personal, intimate, and mysterious events of our lives. The voices around us say, "Keep going. People come and go, change and stay the same, grow old and die, but you must continue to go on as if the there is no tomorrow." Country songs and needlepoint pillows encourage us to "Live like you are dying." We are obedient to these voices, running on autopilot. Yet these days I sense a growing urge to experience more fully our losses. The phrase to "live like you're dying" has some desperation in it that I don't think is helpful. So instead, I suggest you rewrite that phrase and "die like you are living" because no matter what kind of death you are experiencing, you will go on to live in this world or the next.

> The listening part of a goodbye is as important as the speaking part of the goodbye.

When you experience a loss or when you need to make an exit, you have to relearn life. Experiences that were familiar will feel like the first time because who or what use to accompany them is absent. Now they feel uncertain and undefined. You experience the first Mother's Day without mom, the first Christmas in a wheelchair, the first party since the divorce, the first week without a paycheck, the first time you need to use glasses. You can no longer predict how you will feel. Familiar occasions have become strangely unfamiliar. You thought you only had to say goodbye once, but there is an ongoing feeling that what has left keeps leaving. After you say goodbye to your spouse at the cemetery you say goodbye again when your grandchild's wedding invitation asks you to RSVP for single or "plus one." It is another reminder that there is no plus one anymore. Goodbye, again.

Does time heal our acceptance of hard goodbyes? Does time heal the pain of growing old and death? Not the way we want it to. When we say goodbye to a true love, the pain is seldom healed by time. The longer we live without them, the more fully aware we are of all that we lost. When we say goodbye to the stages of our life as we change and grow old, the days stack up one after the other, and we become more and more aware of what we are living without.

It is easier to talk about goodbyes when we are in the midst of beginnings. When we are young and healthy, we are comfortable talking about growing old and dying. When we are employed or married, it is easier to discuss unemployment or being single. It doesn't matter if we are at the beginning or end, at twenty-five or eighty-five, we must meditate on and contemplate loss. It's imperative. To go through life looking only for the good times is a dangerous life, not just unsatisfying. We must embrace the mountaintops with the valleys and live in the totality of our lives. Too many of us live as if sitting on the fifty-yard line of a stadium. It is a safe place with a good view, but the best parts of the game are in the end zones. So too, our lives are uninspiring and mind-numbing from that position. Or we live on the merry go-round, where life is predictable but goes nowhere. The roller coaster has its downsides but finds momentum in the climb. Too many of us avoid the color black, but as any artist knows, only by adding black into the painting will the richness and drama manifest on the canvas. We have the tendency to avoid or deny the painful sides of life. To live fully we must embrace both our beginnings and our ends where we begin again. Embrace the fullness of life and contemplate loss so that you can appreciate victories.

We know and love so many people that have made the final exit from this earth. This is the most sacred exit practice of all. Deep love does not allow for complete exits from earth because real love is forever. Love does not accept limitations of hours or weeks, even centuries. If our deepest loved one dies, their exit is never completely accepted. Here's what I have learned: The same love that hates endings allows us to accept beginnings. Love is the basis for grief AND hope. The more fully we love, the more fully we believe that true love, true survival, has no restrictions or limitations, not even of death. Our survival invites us to reconsider all that threatens it. We discover that in every ending there is a beginning.

Growing old, getting sick, and the exit through physical death is hard for us. Too often it is connected to weakness and failure. Such exits open us to a new dimension that is a kind of surrender. This is the great paradox in life. We end things in order to begin. The greatest power is to be able to surrender ourselves in our exits. They are the opportunity to experience powerlessness, which is the experience of being God-guided.

If I have given you the impression that exits are easy, I do not mean to. Exits are not easy. Perishing, leaving, and good-byes are something that we will most likely protest with every breath. It is the opposite of most kinds of survival. Even Christ did not want to exit this earth. He never spoke about death as something he wanted, and He knew the purpose of His death. We see His deep agony and distress. His sweat fell to the ground as blood. He cried out, "Why have you deserted me?" This removes any romantic illusions of the exit of death. We must prepare for loss and exits (but we will still be a little unprepared.)

As I reflect on the way we make our exits, I see clearly the kind that are sacred and the kind that are not. Poor goodbyes that hang on for the wrong reasons or to the wrong parts of a relationship or situation do not belong to God. Sacred exits believe that in every end there is a beginning. In God there is no ending. God is a God of creation and life, so we feel the pain because endings feel unnatural. Some endings are absurd, if only because we are created for life. I always struggled when people would say to me, "If you really believe in heaven you will not mourn people exiting this world and passing on to the next." But, oh no, it is because I believe and celebrate LIFE that I protest. This is the miracle of my faith: that God knows the full absurdity of death, died as all men will, and threw it off in resurrection.

Exits hold power for us. If we change our perspective of exits from defeat to celebration, we change our survival journey to anticipation and completeness. Exits change us. They don't account for our whole life, but they do define us because they further our transformation to wholeness. We develop new beginnings and new lives. We stop competing. We stop comparing. We stop waiting and postponing life. We learn from our goodbyes. We face our fears. We start living in new beginnings instead of living in the goodbye. For better or worse, we find ways to become more than our goodbye. Sacred exits can help us find our way back to who God created us to be.

## THOUGHTS TO CONTEMPLATE ABOUT EXITS

1. What is one goodbye that you never got to say growing up? Write that goodbye now.

2. Who said goodbye to you without you being able to respond? Write that goodbye now.

3. What do you need to exit to enter a new phase of your life? What does a good goodbye look and sound like for this situation? Write about it now.

NOTES:

# CHAPTER TEN

# Decisions

Over the past nine chapters, we've seen how Sacred Survival turns the promise of God's abundant life into a
practice. Sacred Survival makes a different kind of promise to us from the ordinary assurance that "life goes on." It
promises us that we can be more than barely alive. Life can
be beautiful. Even if you're a guy that doesn't typically think
of his life in the context of "beautiful," I appeal to you to re
frame your existence as a wonderfully appealing and capti-
vating life (other words for beautiful). The most Sacred Survival is founded on authentic, true stories of life in the wake
of loss, with strength, awareness, and acceptance, through
compassion and relationships, amid exits that lead to new
decisions. This kind of survival challenges and changes not
just your life, but everyone's life around you.

The practices of Sacred Survival don't make your life matter, because your life already does; only now you can believe
and feel like it does. Sacred Survival is ultimately about your

true unique story and how you tell your story. Survivals that matter uncover their true experiences and share them thoughtfully and compassionately. To claim your Sacred Survival on earth, you have to make the connection between you, this world, and the eternity you live for. This connection is called truth. Living in truth always demands decisions that can be easy but often are difficult.

The last practice in your sacred survival is making new decisions that flow in and out of the other five practices. These decisions are tangible and intangible. They include material choices about relationships, jobs, and health, as well as the subtle decisions that bring trust, respect, hope, and dignity into your life.

## YOUR TRUE STORY—PAST, PRESENT, AND FUTURE

We don't always have the ability to make the right choices but we do have the ability to change our decisions and amend our plans and practices. Altering our lives is about seeking and finding new ways to approach the decisions in our lives. That is, we need to change more than our decisions; we need to change the very way we approach making our decisions. The best approach is through the door of truth. Your decisions are best when they are based on your true story filled with your real-life experiences, not anyone else's. Your true story is constantly being written, and it is the only thing that is truly unique. Only you have lived your life the way you have. With each accumulating experience you develop a life that is the only one of its kind. Of course, we have many things in common and find hope in seeing how others live when we recognize similar trials and troubles. And we may hold some eternal and absolute truths in the universe. But the beginning of enlightenment is in the absence of comparing ourselves to others, or living another's life, or wearing another's decisions like a clever costume instead of owning a custom-made, first-rate choice.

A Sacred Survival must constantly account, accept, adjust, and allow for the truth that uniquely fits YOU. That sounds so simple—just be true to yourself. Know your true feelings. Find your true purpose. Well, if it is so simple, why are so many people barely alive? As we have discussed, it could be that we don't believe in ourselves. We are afraid that our own lives aren't as good as what we see on TV or what we hear about in our circle of friends. Too often we look at the way other people survive and think, "If I 'do' life just like they do, I will end up with their life, which at this moment looks better than mine." But things are rarely what they appear to be.

We learn the hard way that building a survival plan on a false image is not sustainable. Powerful lives that built their existence on image and splashy egotistical strategies crumble. They tried to demonstrate their vitality with size and force. Every day we read about people who have been pretending to be someone they are not. We find out that they have falsified college transcripts and work histories and created diplomas and W-2 forms with sophisticated graphic design. Correctional institutions are filled with people pretending to be someone else instead of surviving by their own truths. We imprison ourselves when we lock away our true identity behind a life of deception or betrayal.

Sacred Survival asks you to forget about image and proving you're okay. It's not about appearances; it's about authenticity. You have a story that no one else has. Only you have experienced it. It pushes and pulls you to survive. As we said at the beginning of the book, the world loves survival stories, especially the ones that describe uncompromised success and beating the odds, because they resonate with our instinct to live. Now, embrace your decisions within the framework of the practices you have discovered:

1. You have unique strength that you already possess.
2. You have thoughts and feelings about losses that require acceptance and continual adjustments.
3. Compassion is the language of God that unifies us and renews your strength.
4. You are created for supernatural relationships that will sustain and improve your survival.
5. Life is a series of letting go and going on. The right kind of exits can be your best beginning.
6. Your decisions turn the promise of a Sacred Survival into a practice.

The combined practices of strength, acceptance, compassion, relationships, exits, and decisions will turn your survival into a Sacred Survival. They are founded on the events in your life that have been twisting through your survival journey. Recurring events in your life have shaped your values and beliefs, and they can push you forward or hold you back. Are your decisions holding you back or moving you forward?

> The practices of Sacred Survival don't make your life matter, because your life already does matters; only now you can believe and feel like it does.

The way you carry out your practices not only reflects your current state of beliefs, but also shapes what you believe about your future survival.

Your past is a powerful force in your life, for better or worse. With all its power, it must not control you, but it can give you clues to define your authentic survival. While life goes on, you must confront the negative beliefs that past experiences have programmed in your mind. You might begin by asking if your memories are a work of fiction that you have falsely created or someone else's version of reality. Figure this out so that you can begin again on the right pathway. How can you survive your future if you don't know the truth of your past and present?

## START AT THE RIGHT END OF THE DECISION

Too many survivals start at the wrong end of the journey. People imagine what they want their lives to look like, and then they try to wiggle into someone else's plan. Goals and objectives are important, but consider starting at the other end of the journey. From that position ask yourself who you were when you were created. No matter how many times I ask that question, respondents seem unsure how to answer. Typically they go to third-person-scriptures foretelling the fulfillment of God's plan or to anecdotes describing the hopes and dreams of their parents. But if you dig a little deeper into your "once upon a time" story, you will be reminded that you were created whole, complete, full of value, and fully human. "I'm only human" shouldn't be an excuse for poor behavior or disappointing results. It is, instead, an exclamation of power and God's image.

You were originally created for good works and great things. Knowing this means you don't have to go looking for what makes your survival sacred. The truth already lies within you. You are already valuable, whether you think you "made something of yourself" or lost who you once were. The plot of my story, perhaps like yours, has been complicated and gone from fairy tale, to horror story, to action adventure, to its current chapter of happily ever after. One of the first lessons in survival is to understand that who we are on the outside often misrepresents who we are created to be on the inside. If we don't reconcile our inner selves with our outward living, we create a tension that can quite literally eat a hole in us. Our true identity wants to get out!

## BE YOUR BEST

The next decision you have to make is to be your best. After envisioning who you are in the context of sharing your true story, think about what it means to be your best. Being your best is different than doing your best. When you "do" life, you are performance-driven, trying to make ourselves or others feel better about who you are. It is like putting the cart before the horse or the tail wagging the dog. Instead, when you let yourself fully experience your best God-given qualities, you can't help but manifest them in meaningful ways. For example, when you experience your compassionate natures you will do acts of kindness. When you feel your worthiness, you will give others respect. When you feel how whole you are, you will offer others justice and honesty. The more you sink into who you are, the more you express who you are with what you do. The decision to be your best starts with acknowledging the best qualities we all possess made in the image of God.

Being your best will look different every day. No day is the same because a life of survival is a life of continual change and adjustment. Today you may be sick, but you can be your best even if you cannot do things as well as yesterday. Today you may be sad but you can be your best to be loving and honest even while acknowledging your pain and sorrow. Today you may be alone, but you can be your best in your home alone in your thoughts and moments of contemplation. Being your best doesn't compare your life to another's. Your best may not be in the form of an endeavor. It is more about being than doing. This is a difficult shift to make in your survival that has been based on trying harder and harder to do better and better.

Why are we caught in this performance-driven life? From a very early age we begin earning our way through life. As soon as we experience disappointment from our parents, teachers, or anyone important in our life we think, "What do I have to do to make them happy?" Our lives are set on a trajectory of performing and pleasing in order to make everyone happier, calmer, and sometimes less abusive. We stop BEING who we are and DOING what we think will control the outcome of our lives. Life becomes a complicated chess game of plotting our next move in anticipation of how the world will respond to us.

One of the most sacred decisions you can make is to be your best without trying to control anyone's response. Being your best means, simply, being your best in spirit and intention, which will manifest in acts of thoughtfulness and kindness. Being your best gives up the excuses, apathy, and belief that good is good enough. Being your best shows up in a healthier, happier life and a Sacred Survival.

## BE PERSONAL WITHOUT TAKING IT PERSONALLY

Making a decision to be more personal will make a meaningful difference in your life. This is different from taking what happens to you personally. I know they sound like the same thing, but making it personal, and taking it personally are worlds apart. Making my life personal means I interact with people and places in special ways and remove the barriers that create distance between us. I try to connect with everyone and everything with eye contact, a pat on the back, handwritten notes, phone calls instead of texts, going inside instead of driving through, getting more face time instead of logging more Facebook. I try to set aside everything from electronics to attitudes that make my relationships less personal.

When I buy someone a gift, I make it personal by thinking about what would make them happy. I personally pick something out based on their wants and needs, handwrite a note that shows I know them, and deliver it in a way that brings attention to them and not me. I try to connect with them on an emotional level. I try to touch that person physically, emotionally, and spiritually. That's all I can control and be responsible for. Sometimes their reaction is over the top, and they cheer and applaud me. And sometimes people complain and criticize me no matter what I do. I don't take their reaction personally. Their response says more about them and where they are in their journey than it says about me and my journey. I believe their attitude points back to who they are, based on what they've gone through. This is the difference between making it personal and taking it personally. The decision to be personal attempts to create closeness while taking things personally is self-centered or confusing. A Sacred Survival decides to move towards each other where you will be uniquely rewarded.

> If we don't reconcile our inner selves with our outward living, we create a tension that can quite literally eat a hole in us. Our true identity wants to get out!

## ENGAGE YOUR WHOLE SELF IN YOUR DECISIONS

This next decision is complex and multifaceted. Far more decisions are made than are ever executed in our lives. We put so much time into deliberating and tweaking our decisions or waiting for the right time to carry them out, that we run out of energy before we actually implement them. We mistake the passion of the decision for actual accomplishment. For your decisions to matter, you must engage both emotion and motion. You must take the decision into your entire body. If it is only an intellectual decision, your heart will not ignite it into action. You need to put your heart in it, or you'll grow weary quickly. And if it's only a heartfelt decision, your head can talk you out of it.

> We mistake the passion of the decision for actual accomplishment. For your decisions to matter, you must engage both emotion and motion.

Each day we make thousands upon thousands of voluntary and involuntary decisions. Some lose steam the minute we announce them. Some of the decisions to move forward are never acted on because we tell ourselves that we can't do it, we don't deserve it, or we will surely fail. But setting the big ones in motion—the ones about the purpose of life—is how we can turn endings into beginnings. Every end can be reworked toward fulfilling your purpose. A Sacred Survival integrates your spiritual, physical, and emotional self into making and executing your decisions.

## BE AWARE

We have so many voices in our heads telling us what we cannot do. The voice of pain is so selfish and loud that it blurs our vision and thwarts our goals. It distorts our awareness from what's important to what's urgent. The voice of truth tells a different story. It says, "See, feel, hear, and know that a life with pain clarifies what is most important." Once aware of this voice, listen and believe in it. Practicing awareness creates possibilities, and when we have possibilities, we can live a life of purpose. That is, without possibilities we have no choice, and without choice we live without passion.

Awareness is the beginning of change into a Sacred Survival because it informs you of new choices. Decide to listen to your thoughts. Get in touch with your feelings. Notice your reactions. Do you think and feel like running, distracting, numbing, protecting, or arguing? Ironically, we survive better when we allow ourselves to acknowledge and lean into the pain that threatens our survival. In this position, we cry out and are heard by the one who will meet us with compassion. Compassion will carry some of our pain so we can carry out our decisions. But this process begins with awareness of our pain, hopes, wants, and needs. Awareness helps us pull all the practices together. This process can play out in an instant or in a lifetime of moments connected by a lifestyle of Sacred Survival.

## WHERE DO YOU FEEL THE PRESENCE OF SACRED PRACTICES?

I made some important decisions a few years ago about my work, health, and relationships—otherwise known as the big New Year's Resolutions. Maybe you've made these kinds of decisions, too. I decided to go back to school, increase my physical activity, spend more time with my parents, spend less time with impersonal acquaintances, and discover the training of Qigong. All of these decisions were based on adjustments I was making as my youth, health, and physical mobility declined. My tangible losses were obvious. I was fifty-five, my health was changing, and my relationships never felt more precious. The intangible, ambiguous losses were harder to uncover. I had lost my self-confidence, some relationships, security, my ego, and the life I thought I was going to have. Guided by who I knew I was created to be (whole and valuable), I didn't make the kind of decisions that would send me on an elusive treasure hunt. I knew that the treasure of God's value was already inside of me. To help me adjust to the uncertainty of my life, I needed to uncover the richness inside me and apply my God-given strengths that would allow me to live out my decisions. But emotional and physical pain was blurring my vision and weakening my efforts. I wasn't surviving well. I was in a kind of hell.

Then I met the girl with sparkly ruby-red slippers. I was sitting in my wheelchair at the big Hobby Lobby because I was tired and hurting. I've observed a lot of different reactions to my chair, or more accurately, to me in my chair. What stands out is the difference between a child's reaction and an adult's reaction. Invariably, I get respect. Typically, adults will look past me or give me a polite "excuse me" as they go around me. But children, oh, they are perfectly honest. At the Hobby Lobby, a little girl that looked about four years old walked right up to me. She had big eyes and ruby-red shoes with sequin sparkles. She leaned in close, put her hand on my knee, and said, "Honey, what happened to you?" I smiled, surprised at her candid question. I explained that on some days I was too tired to walk, but that I was happy and fine. "Do you hurt?" she asked. I nodded yes. Then she did something so simple and so profound. She patted my knee and said, "There, there."

In that moment I felt incredible compassion. She personified powerful innocence that comes with childhood. When I think about the words of Jesus, "I tell you the truth, unless you change and become like children you will never enter the kingdom of heaven," I just can't wait for His kingdom to come, on earth as it is in heaven. I wish we all had her childlike trust and openness that wants to connect and be personal with even a stranger in a wheelchair.

In the innocence of her childhood, she didn't overlook me, look down on me, or tell me what I needed to do. I didn't have to explain or defend myself. I wasn't any less than, better than, or different from her. We were united in that beautiful moment of compassion. Her two kind words had volumes of influence over me. That little girl carried some of my pain so I wasn't burdened with it all. And as I was freed from carrying it all, I could carry on, differently, and better in that difference. I felt better.

The little girl with the red sparkly slippers didn't know it, but she helped me carry out my decisions. Her acceptance reminded me that I could accept myself. She brought her innate strength of relating to people into my life and made me feel strong and alive. That awareness helped me leave behind the version of myself filled with doubt and insecurity. And perhaps, most importantly, she reminded me that we cannot survive well when we isolate and try to make it alone. In an instant she was using all the Sacred Survival practices and changing my survival from bearable that day to beautiful.

Where are the ruby slippers in your life? We all find God's presence differently. You may feel His presence in music, in nature, in groups

> Practicing awareness creates possibilities, and when we have possibilities, we can live a life of purpose.

of friends, or in quiet contemplation. You may see the face of God in the face of a four-year-old at the Hobby Lobby.

We all make decisions that range from easy to difficult. At some level they all require energy, resources, time, and intention. But even if we had infinite amounts of these, we face the voices in our head telling us that our decisions are too hard, we're not good enough, and the risks are not worth it. These messages hold us back. We try to survive by filling up the voids in our life instead of reclaiming the wholeness inside of us. The physical and emotional pain we carry is too heavy for us to carry anything else. We have been laying down the wrong thing—our decisions instead of our pain. Stand up for your decisions. Even in a wheelchair I can stand up for what is right.

There are a lot of great songs written and sung to us about home: leaving home, coming home, searching for home. Home is important to us. When we are stranded on our proverbial island trying to survive, we hold on to the hope that we will get home. Sometimes this is a physical place, and sometimes it is a place in our heart, mind, or soul. Most of us know the classic song "Somewhere Over the Rainbow" from *The Wizard of Oz*. It resonates with our lives of chasing hopes and dreams. At the end of the story, we are invited to see that we don't have to look over the rainbow for our dreams to come true. We learn that there is no place like home. One of my favorite songs about home is an Amy Grant song called "In a Little While." In this song her words hold out comfort for those surviving a life of trouble and pain. She offers the comfort that, in a little while, we'll be "home" forever. I used to long for that, hoping I could hold on just a little longer for what I believed my final homecoming would be: heaven. But these last years as I practiced a Sacred Survival I've stopped waiting for a "little while" and realized that I am already home. I had been looking over the rainbow instead of recognizing that my true home is inside me where my God is and where strength comes from. Many feel stranded, longing to get home. They remain isolated from acceptance, compassion, and relationships. Sacred Survival invites them (and urges you) to exit and decide to live a different kind of life, now.

## NOW

Your next decision is to begin the six practices of Sacred Survival. Now is the time. There is no moment more important than this moment we know as NOW. You may have been too tired or scared, too disappointed, or too angry to think about your survival. You have wanted a better life so badly but you didn't allow yourself to hope. The possibility of losing was too threatening. You have ended up going it alone rather than risking the humiliation of a public defeat. That isolation began to define you, and your survival has been a constant struggle. When I asked hundreds of people what inspires them, invariably they focused on people's struggles more than the happy ending. Oh we want the happy ending, and I want it for you. But what inspires us is the struggle. Your struggle inspires me. Your struggle is proof that you are created for life and that you haven't given up.

> There is no moment more important than this moment we know as NOW.

At this moment, the most important decision you will ever make as a survivor is to believe that your life matters. These six practices won't make it so; they will affirm that it does. A Sacred Survival isn't just showing up in life. It is a practice, practice, practice. You may be genuinely surprised when you survive! But soak it in because it is validation of all you are. No one else can do it for you. Your Sacred Survival already exits inside you. Your rescue begins now.

## THOUGHTS TO CONTEMPLATE ABOUT DECISIONS

1. What is the difference between being your best and doing your best?

2. Which way leads your decision-making? Thinking, feeling, believing? How can you integrate these powers in your life to be fully engaged in your decisions?

3. Which of the sacred practices seems to be the most important to carry out your decisions?

4. What rules in your life hold you back from implementing decisions?

5. What moves you forward to put your decisions into action?

6. What is the next decision in your life? How will you be your best and be fully engaged? How will you make this a personal goal without taking people's reactions personally?

NOTES:

# THE END

## THE BEGINNING